Socialization to Politics

Basic Concepts in Political Science

SOCIALIZATION
TO POLITICS

DEAN JAROS

PRAEGER PUBLISHERS
New York · Washington

BOOKS THAT MATTER

Published in the United States of America in 1973
by Praeger Publishers, Inc.
111 Fourth Avenue, New York, N.Y. 10003

Library of Congress Catalog Card Number: 70–189911

Printed in the United States of America

Contents

1. The Concept of Political Socialization

Politics in the modern world has sometimes been described as a battle for men's minds. Although this cliché is melodramatic, there is a strong element of truth in it. To even the most casual observer of public affairs it is now clear that what happens in politics is not a simple consequence of constitutional decree, law, formal guarantee, or institutional form. Constitutions may look nice on paper and subscribe to the logic of well-meaning planners, but too often they do not work: witness the fate of the republican regime of Germany after World War I. One may legislate against corruption, but that alone will not make it go away: witness the antiparty, reform legislation of the United States during the late nineteenth and early twentieth centuries. Much the same is true at the international level: witness the formal regulations of the United Nations, which need not govern delegate behavior at critical junctures. The list is endless.

The point is obvious: political behavior is governed by norms, consciences, beliefs, and values. If an institutional form is not appropriate to these human mental phenomena, that institutional form will probably not survive. Presidents are not respected, laws are not obeyed, taxes are not paid, political stability does not prevail—unless people believe. What is true for established institutions is true for revolutionary and iconoclastic movements as well. Barricades are not built, guerrilla leaders are not followed or protected, mass-demonstrations are not attended—unless people believe. The nature of the norms, consciences, etc., determines what the nature of all politics shall be; who shall have power and who shall not depends upon the support of the masses of citizens. Because the stakes are so high, it is not surprising that so large and so varied a group should be vying for political support. We see evidence of this every day. We are urged to vote for a particular alternative. We are urged to support the President's policy. Newspapers editorialize on the perfidious nature of an incumbent. Firebrands urge revolution. The mass media create political images. Television vividly portrays all features of American life—and creates new political demands. Traditionally liberal college professors indoctrinate their students —much to the distress of traditionally conservative community notables. These are all examples of attempts to win men's minds. All are based on the premise that political behavior is governed by values and norms.

If the nature of politics is determined by the political behavior people exhibit, and if behavior is dependent upon norms and consciences, the next obvious question is, What determines the norms and consciences? Some of the answers we have just hinted at: campaign propaganda, government communications, newspapers, public speeches, and television. There is no question that these are important; indeed, considerable research is being done to determine exactly what their effect is.

But over and above these, we must entertain the possibility that what people do in politics depends upon what they learn about it while they are still children. Children continuously receive training or education or indoctrination. Such is the nature of child rearing. That some of the training or education or indoctrination may have political components seems highly likely; thus, we may ask whether political norms may be developed at a tender age and then persist into adulthood. The tremendous implications of this possibility have resulted in the recent development of a whole new area of study. In the last few years, the term *political socialization* has been increasingly used to refer to these youthful learning processes. Prior to 1960, no one used this term; by the 1970's anyone who had any connection with political science not only recognized it, but was expected to deal with the idea. The prospects of finding the roots of patriotism or revolution, of stability or instability in the operation of the political system, of success or failure in the process of political development, to say nothing of differential policy preferences and partisan behavior, have attracted both student and professor. Whole courses are devoted to this topic, and books and articles are written about the political development of the young.

But though the term may be new, and the curriculums and books may represent innovations, the idea of attaining or retaining political power by controlling the minds of men has been a tantalizing possibility for centuries, whether by transmitting political knowledge or information (a process we shall call *cognitive socialization*) or communicating political beliefs and values (a process we shall call *affective socialization*). Anthropologists and historians tell us that the wielders of political power have always been concerned with indoctrinating the young in order to secure continuing political loyalty and promote governmental stability. Educators observe that all countries have had programs of civic training. These efforts certainly transmit to children at least a smattering of *knowledge* about politics and at the same time expose them to norms that support the regime and glorify political heroes of a bygone era. Of course, revolutionary leaders, too, have sought to indoctrinate the young, believing that subversive and iconoclastic contempt for established institutions must likewise be learned. Lenin was too skilled an architect of strategy to leave the training of his future cadres merely to chance and circumstance.

It seems obvious that whether it be holding forks or saluting flags, regular behavior patterns are not mystically transmitted. They don't just happen; they are learned. Indeed, this principle is a classic concern of politics. The new study of political socialization thus does not represent the discovery of a new problem. It is more accurate to say that attention has been refocused on one of the venerable and enduring questions of political life.

CLASSICAL THOUGHT

The seminal work on the promotion of political stability through indoctrination is undoubtedly Plato's *Republic*. The great emphasis in the *Republic* on making the young into good citizens through extremely comprehensive state-run instructional programs is so impressive that many think education, not politics, was Plato's chief concern.

Plato believed there was only one best state;[1] it was the terrestrial reflection of the divine Idea, or Form, of the state. Once this best state was achieved, any change in its character would necessarily involve degeneration. For Plato, therefore, the ideal state must be a stable state, and stability is achieved by perfecting mechanisms of social control. The way in which change is to be avoided is to teach the citizens to accept their proper roles in society, to act out the "innate differences which fit them for different occupations."[2] Men are to be taught to occupy their distinct places in a rigid status hierarchy. The citizens of the Republic are to be so indoctrinated as to limit their aspirations to what is justly theirs and to ensure they will be happy in their social positions. Without proper education and training, men will soon develop improper ambitions. Conflict will result, changes in the relations among men will begin, and the ideal state will decay. "Such interference and exchange of social positions . . . would be fatal to the commonwealth."[3] To prevent the change-producing clash of ambitions, one must begin the political socialization process early, for "when children have made a good beginning . . . and . . . education has instilled a spirit of order, this reverence for law . . . will attend them in all their doings . . . restoring any institutions that may earlier have fallen into decay."[4] Much of the *Republic* is taken up with prescribing the proper training patterns for various classes in the proposed ideal state. Given Plato's assumptions, small wonder he discusses education so thoroughly. Without proper political indoctrination all is lost.

Plato is hardly unique among the ancients in recognizing the importance of political socialization. Confucius and other Eastern scholars also considered political socialization to be of crucial importance in securing the stability of regimes. Not only a philosopher and scholar, Confucius was actively engaged in politics as an adviser to princes. Although historians of the era stress the role of conspiracy, treachery, and violence, Confucius scorned control by coercion and force.[5] He suggested to various

Chinese provincial rulers that they bolster their insecure political positions by seeking to train better citizens. Centuries before modern scholars began to investigate the linkage between family life and political attitudes, Confucius emphasized "filial piety," believing that the sentiments of love and respect a youngster feels toward his parents will in later life extend to men in positions of political authority. Order in political life crucially depends on a well-regulated family life.[6] It is to be noted that the process of social indoctrination that Confucius prescribes depends only marginally on formal or direct education. The family, or patriarch, does not directly inculcate the substantive beliefs that will lead to political stability. It is more important to implant the proper generalized attitudes of respect than it is specifically to teach children to "honor the prince." Subsequently, political authority becomes the object of these attitudes.

Turning to more recent thinkers, we find St. Thomas More and Jean-Jacques Rousseau, both architects of utopian communities, echoing Plato in stressing the necessity of childhood socialization. Both would communicate as much knowledge to children as possible. But, said St. Thomas, cognitive socialization is not enough. In *Utopia,*

> [Teachers] use very great endeavor and diligence to put into the heads of their children while they yet be tender and pliant, good opinions and profitable for the conservation of their weal public. Which when they be once rooted in children do remain with them all their life after, and be wondrous profitable for the defense and maintenance of the state of the commonwealth, which never decayeth but through vices rising of evil opinions.[7]

Rousseau also insists that the young be affectively socialized; "intensification of social sentiment" is a goal to be pursued. Although in *The Social Contract* Rousseau attacked the existing order as artificial, he was not so foolish as to think that his new, more "naturally" organized society would automatically operate in perfect harmony. The citizens were to be trained to conformity. *The Social Contract* requires the legislator to indoctrinate political values almost continuously. Although the general will is sovereign, the whole people cannot really legislate for itself without prior instruction. The citizens, "[a]ll have equally a need for guidance. [They] must be *taught* what it is they will. From this increase of public *knowledge* would result . . . harmony . . . and the highest power of the whole." [8] Rousseau many times under-scores his belief that it is education of the young that provides the foundation for social life. Finally, in "Considerations on the Government of Poland," his most specific words on political indoctrination of the young: "It is *education* that must give souls a national formation, and direct their opinions and tastes in such a way that they will be patriotic by inclination, by passion, by necessity." [9] Rousseau stands out as one of the most enthu-siastic advocates of childhood political indoctrination.

To a modern liberal, the passages on the preceding pages sound menacing, for they speak of ways to achieve effective social control by indoctrinating the helpless young. These practices differ from those suggested by Aldous Huxley in the anti-utopia of *Brave New World* only in degree and sophistication. Huxley foresees total control achieved by complete genetic and environ-mental manipulation of the young.[10] Far from being unique, the bizarre human production laboratories he envisioned are but a logical extension of notions that have agitated political theorists for thousands of years.

POLITICAL POWER HOLDERS

Joining these scholars in their concern with the relation of childhood indoctrination to social control are political rulers of every type and description whose fortunes are immediately bound up with political stability. All regimes invest heavily in formal or informal educational programs, and one output of educational programs is social indoctrination. Attempts to perpetuate belief in the legitimacy of political forms and to encourage respect for prevailing political values have had a long history. What ancient regime has not glorified its tradition? What revolutionary cadre has not railed against the received normative doctrine, has not tried to build a tradition of the new, to apotheosize itself? Examples come readily to mind.

The education program of the Soviet Union has long intrigued Western observers. The deliberate and unconcealed political purposes that the entire educational and state-run child care systems are made to serve show the faith the Soviets maintain in the possibility of manipulating minds while they are yet young. The formal school system is directed to advance the purposes of those in authority. The program, all-inclusive as it is, seeks to transmit both political commitment and information. As one eminent scholar has put it, "values, beliefs, and the individual's view of life and society have been shaped within the desired ideological and political molds, but, at the same time, the individual has been permitted to accumulate objective knowledge for practical ends." [11] The educational program produces not only technically skilled citizens but loyal subjects as well. But childhood socialization extends far beyond the formal educational system. Party youth organizations—the Little Octobrists, Young Pioneers, and the Communist Youth League—are designed not only to instill loyalty to the regime but, like Plato's academy for philosopher-kings, also to train future party elites in the skills of leadership.[12] In some areas, the program of indoctrination is supplemented by organizing many other childhood activities, like hobbies, music, and recreation.[13] The attempt to occupy all of an individual's activities in hopes of precluding alternate sources of influence is an ancient technique. Thus, the very great importance that Lenin put on conditioning the young to accept Soviet rule, on "teaching Communism" as a prerequisite to the survival of the regime,[14] has been fully honored in Soviet practice.

A similar confidence in the power of childhood indoctrination to mold the contours of society was expressed by Adolf Hitler's Nazi regime.[15] His plan for elevating Germans to a hysterical, expansionist enthusiasm included an extensive program of "educating the masses." The program included children, as well as the adults who could directly participate in military and paramilitary activity. As early as 1934, school literature that emphasized military exploits, heroism, and, of course, nationalism was prescribed.[16] Educational materials were drastically and immediately changed to encourage the new militaristic spirit of the German state, especially at the elementary school level. Teachers were "coordinated" in various ways. There was, of course, institutional reorganization to facilitate "national political training";[17] but in addition, dismissals, threats, and coercion forced a pro-Nazi, or at least submissive, attitude among educators. Teacher training was standardized and tightly controlled, with new candidates for teaching positions carefully screened for proper political views.[18] Apart from the formal education system, the Nazis attempted to neutralize competing sources of socialization by establishing state-operated youth leagues, recreation programs, and the like. Even entertainment was used as a vehicle for political indoctrination; films were censored and "objectionable" music was proscribed.[19]

The Third Reich had not yet finally collapsed when the victorious powers began to think about how to cope with what the Nazi socialization program had wrought. The answer was a counterindoctrination of youth in order to implant new, democratic political values.[20] In fact, the Allied occupation of Germany represented a period of considerable educational censorship. In what has been described as an orgy of book burning, many textbooks were rejected because they were contaminated by Nazi beliefs.[21] Teachers, most of whom had been members of the Nazi party, were thoroughly screened before they were licensed to teach in the classroom. Reacting to the shortage their censorship had created, Allied occupation authorities began, after the war, to supervise the development of new texts for German children and to establish teacher training institutes in an attempt to qualify enough politically reliable people to staff the schools.[22] Other institutions that might serve a political socialization function, such as youth groups, were quickly set up. The athletic and cultural activities did attract German youth, and it was hoped that their contact with Allied personnel would have an impact on their conduct "and assist in the reconstruction of German youth."[23]

The governments set up after the end of Allied occupation were equally determined to exclude Nazi thought from educational practice.[24] Indeed, the continuing concern for the political orientation of German youth and its implications for future German government shows how salient a matter the political indoctrination of youth had by then become.[25]

Political indoctrination, though perhaps in less dramatic form, is also to be found in more democratic nations. Civic education programs in the United States are cases in point. Public educators attract both praise and blame for their efforts to socialize the young both affectively and cognitively. New programs designed to buttress the young against the influence of Communism and intense battles over the use of textbooks allegedly written by persons of questionable political ideals serve to highlight the educator's political role and to emphasize the prevalent belief that direct indoctrination during childhood has important political consequences.[26] Although outright jingoism is probably on the way out, there can be no doubt that educators attempt to create appropriate political attitudes. At a minimum, they lay great stress on the virtues of democracy and encourage democratic participation in the affairs of government.[27]

The political indoctrination of children has not been confined to the highly organized modern state. Even the most primitive communities make this a common practice. In such societies, political indoctrination doubtless depends more on "informal" socialization, but to say that it is informal does not imply that it is casual. Families, in particular, are vehicles for the steady transmission of political tradition, practices, and beliefs, but some formal community functions—such as evening storytelling hours and ceremonies—are always dramatic devices for socializing the young to become functioning members of the adult community.[28] Among the Chaga of East Africa, for example, the family instills awe and reverence for the chief. There is much explicit instruction in proper deferential behavior and forms of address. The importance and almost superhuman qualities of the chief are continuously impressed upon the child. He is made to watch ceremonies in the home where the chief and his emissaries are honored. In short, the child is continually bombarded with examples and precepts that tell him to respect the chief and his authority.[29] Primitive initiation ceremonies and puberty rites compel respect and veneration for social authority.[30] The rites usually include threats of dire consequences to be administered by man or god should the initiate violate any tribal prescriptions. But the Mende of Sierra Leone are perhaps the most explicit in including political socialization features in their initiations. As part of a lengthy and terrible ceremony (several weeks involving the application of scar markings, beatings, and other terrifying ordeals) respect for law and political custom is instilled by holding mock government sessions in which the boys play the parts of the appropriate political figures.[31]

Modern holders of political power use techniques that differ only in degree of elaboration and sophistication from those just discussed. Doubtless these leaders too are the residuary beneficiaries of traditions the family transmits and the norms the family instills. But at the same time they are more active, more comprehensive, and more technically expert in the establishment and sustenance of mechanisms for the direct and formal political indoctrination of youth. Although there is little evidence for the effectiveness of these practices, the very fact that they have existed over such a broad range of time and cultural condition, from primitive tribe to modern superstate, entitles the topic of childhood political learning to serious consideration. It is clear that childhood socialization programs are regarded by political power holders themselves as effective agents in producing loyalty. This notion cannot be ignored.

THE REBIRTH OF POLITICAL SOCIALIZATION: THE FOCI OF CONTEMPORARY RESEARCH

The contemporary political scientist has learned this lesson well. He has taken up the same quest, with a few differences of emphasis. Not being directly involved with those who hold power, today's scholar can afford the luxury of greater contemplation than those caught up in the press of the immediate affairs of state. While the question of loyalty to the regime is clearly important, it is not his sole object of study. The scope of investigation of political socialization has been greatly expanded.

But most importantly, there is much greater interest today in some problems that are largely left implicit or assumed to be obvious in earlier and present nonacademic formulations. These are very basic: (1) what is the impact of political socialization on the political system? and (2) how are critical values learned by children? Is it *really* the case that the state "never decayeth but through vices rising of evil opinions"? Is it *really* the case that "filial piety" leads to respect for political authority? Although the traditional concern with children's political development is rich in ideas, it is unfortunately weak in actual evidence about these ideas. In a very real sense, the efforts of today's empirical political scientists are devoted to correcting this imbalance. This can be accomplished only through research that yields hard information on these two basic questions.

"Systems Effects" or Macro-Level Concerns. If children learn about patriotism, it is reasonable to think that political socialization may have something to do with the fate of nation states. If children learn about political parties and come to believe that some of them are good and others are bad, it is reasonable to think that political socialization may have something to do with the electoral success or failure of parties and perhaps even their survival or demise. If children are taught that change is generally to be regarded with suspicion, political socialization may have something to do with whether, for example, reorganization of government in urban areas is possible. This kind of question —what is the wider institutional impact?—is perhaps the ultimate rationale of political socialization research. There would be little point in studying children's political orientations if their impact on political processes were nil. Although it appears clear that there are some links between what people are taught to believe and the features of political systems, the picture is by no means complete. Exactly what learning leads to a particular regime characteristic remains to be seen, for the most part.

Easton and Dennis, well-known writers in the field of political socialization, express this concern well when they note the necessity of developing a "political theory of political socialization." [32] By political theory, these authors mean a general explanation of the way important political events occur within political systems. How can we account for political stability or revolution, constancy or change? A political theory of political socialization would attempt to specify how political socialization affects these events.

Clearly, *comparative* research is necessary to look at these kinds of problems. If we want to know how socialization affects the fates of nations, we must compare those countries that are strongly supported by their citizens with those that are weak and crumbling because of internal dissension. If the patterns of socialization differ from one class of countries to the other, it may be justifiable to infer an important connection. What little comparative research of this kind that has been done in this area is very exciting and provocative. For example, the question of why partisan politics is stable and placid in some places but volatile and uncertain elsewhere has agitated political scientists for years. The historic experiences of the United States and France are cases in point. The persistence and close competition of Republicans and Democrats for over a century contrasts with the great number and abbreviated tenure of French parties. Interestingly, it has been discovered that patterns of childhood socialization about parties differ greatly in these two countries: most American youngsters are socialized to a party identification at an early age; French children encounter little, if any, party-related socialization.[33] Is there a link here? Is political socialization related to something as basic as the nature of nations' party competition? Of course, we cannot be sure, because other factors may affect party competition. But additional positive evidence of such a role for political socialization has been found as well in comparative studies of several other nations.[34] A connection appears likely.

Political socialization has been regarded as particularly important in the study of the development of the new nations of the world. Clearly, the task of nation building that confronts the recently "liberated" colonial areas involves more than establishing the proper governmental institutions and staffing the administration with competent bureaucrats. It involves the creation of citizens with a commitment to the new nation. It means causing people to subordinate previously important familial, tribal, or religious loyalties to a new national one. Usually, an attempt to deal with this situation is made through a heavy political education program in the schools.[35]

The assumption of many excellent studies is that political socialization programs produce a politically integrated nation, that is, a nation whose citizens are sufficiently homogeneous and sufficiently committed that social decisions can be made and collective tasks undertaken.

> Unless those individuals who are physically and legally members of a political system (that is, who live within its boundaries and are subject to its laws) are also psychologically members of that system (that is, feel themselves to be members), orderly patterns of change are unlikely. It is the sense of identity with the nation that legitimizes the activities of national elites and makes it possible for them to mobilize the commitment and support of their followers.[36]

Clearly very concerned about the system-level effect of socialization, writers making this assumption then go on to describe both the nationalistic orientations and the socialization patterns that they observe.[37] In addition, there are a few studies that actually undertake to determine whether different national developmental patterns are associated with different socialization practices.[38]

Closely related to these problems is the question of the relation of socialization to "type of government" (that is, democratic or nondemocratic). The necessary conditions for democracy have been a topic of speculation for political philosophers, as well as for the research of modern scholars. Though systematic comparison of "democratic" and "nondemocratic" states on the question of socialization has not really been possible, socialization patterns in several countries have been compared. This research has revealed that there are some interesting differences in the way youth learns about norms of participation, feelings of political competence, and other "democratic" orientations.[39] It is worth examining these differences to see if they correspond to our notions of which nations are more, and which less, democratic than others. The results are impressive.[40]

There are a few other areas of research that consider the relationship between patterns of socialization and features of whole countries or communities. For example, one might wonder, is the level of student political demonstration that nations experience due to particular patterns of socialization of youth? A recent study of Taiwan, where there are few student protests, implicitly compared that country with others that have a greater incidence of this kind of disturbance. It was found that Taiwan's students typically undergo a socialization process that increasingly emphasizes security, resignation, and passiveness as they proceed through their education.[41] That these differences in socialization account for national variance in frequency of such demonstrations is quite plausible.

It is clear that we must do a great deal more comparative research if we are to know the political effects of socialization. We do not know much about why nations are democratic, why some cities have more corrupt governments than others, why some states invest heavily in education while others are frugal in this regard, why political change proceeds more easily in some areas than in others, or why some countries are characterized by stability while others are beset by turmoil, coups d'état, and revolution. Political socialization patterns may well be among the clues to what is going on. For centuries men have argued that this is the case. We intuitively feel that it is. We wait on more and better evidence.

Individual or Micro-Level Research. Unfortunately, the kind of research just described is very difficult and very expensive, and, because of this, the progress of knowledge in this field will be extremely slow. But there are many other interesting questions in the field of political socialization. For example, we know that children do in fact acquire political knowledge and political values. How this knowledge and these values are acquired and what the processes of political socialization are excite the curiosity of the modern political scientist. Are the ancient assumptions about proper education and parental influence correct? To what extent does childhood indoctrination work? Do we put aside such fascinating concerns until we have more adequate answers to the question of whether political socialization of youth makes any difference to the polity? Recent scholars have answered no. Despite the lack of evidence, it is plausible to believe that political socialization does make a difference. Much time would be wasted in waiting for conclusive proof. So, political scientists have dug into the question of learning processes and have attempted to explain how youngsters gain their political orientations.

And in fact, these micro-level considerations represent the best-developed areas of research in political socialization. More effort has been devoted to discovering what children know and believe about politics and in investigating the sources of this knowledge and belief than in any other kind of political socialization study. Thus, most of this book will be about micro-level concerns. Greenstein observed that what is, and what ought to be, known about political socialization may be summed up by a single question. "Who learns what from whom under what circumstances with what effects?" [42] Like most other political scientists today, we must leave largely unresolved the "with what effects" part of this paradigm. But we should keep this important question in mind as we learn about who, what, and whom.

Even as we become conscious that this problem hovers over individual-level research, another difficulty with micro-level investigation looms in sight. Suppose we are able to do a thorough investigation of what children, at successive ages, know and believe about politics. Suppose further that we can discover how parental political values leave their imprint on the child. Imagine that we can determine in exactly what areas the civic education programs of the schools are successful and in what areas they fail. Further, we may be able to discover what kinds of political ideas the mass media transmit to the young. If we can accomplish this, we will have made great advances. But in addition to the nagging doubt about how people's political knowledge and preferences affect the way in which political systems function, there is the possibility that *childhood* political orientations have little or no relationship to *adult* political orientations. It is as an adult, of course, that man performs most of his relevant political acts. It is possible that what people learn as children has little relationship to these acts. Things that happen to people as adults may determine adult behavior.

For example, a person may be cynical about government (or trusting of it) because of how he has experienced it as an adult. Did it perform satisfactorily, or did it enact policies that hurt him? Income may be affected by government or some desired services denied. Of course, much of the conventional wisdom about the nature of democracy posits some sort of reciprocal arrangement in which citizens proffer support to government in return for a beneficial syndrome of policy outputs. Who is to say that it is not this dynamic that determines political cynicism or trust rather than childhood teachings about the benevolence or malevolence of public authorities? Indeed, the evidence that this kind of adult experience has some effect on political orientations is convincing.[43] People who live in cities with corrupt governments become cynical. It is thus impossible to argue that youthful political socialization *completely* determines adult political attitudes. The key question is to what extent, *if at all,* do youthful orientations persist to affect later political behavior?

Like the critical matter of the systems-level effects of socialization, answers to this key question require comparative research. However, it is not comparison between systems or nations that we need in this case, but comparisons of the same individuals over time. Put simply, we need to measure people's political orientations while they are children and then again when they are adults. If there are relationships between the two sets of measurements, we are justified in inferring that the childhood orientations persist. If there are no relationships, it appears that childhood socialization is not relevant for adult political behavior and that research in this area is a waste of time.

Of course, as is true for comparative systems-level investigations, there is little evidence of this kind available. Longitudinal research, as it is called, is difficult because it entails keeping track of subjects over many years and reinterviewing them. Such a project might take more than twenty years. Finding the subjects once again and maintaining research interest over such a long period often constitute insurmountable problems.

Despite these problems, some scholars have persevered. In the most well-known political socialization study of this type, the social psychologist Newcomb found that college women were influenced to adopt progressively more "liberal" political attitudes during their college education. This study, performed in the 1930's, demonstrated that college peer groups are important agents of political socialization, an interesting and significant finding in itself.[44] But in addition, Newcomb recently was able to locate the same women who had been students many years earlier. New interviews showed that there were strong relationships between the orientations of college days and those of mature adulthood.[45] Apparently, youthful socialization does persist. There is enough other convincing evidence (not necessarily involving political variables) from longitudinal studies to see that adult attitudes and behavior may generally be a function of earlier orientations.[46] Thus, though more longitudinal work would be desirable, since nothing like a complete picture is at hand, it is possible to undertake studies of the political socialization of youth with a reasonable degree of confidence that they have some relevance to adult behavior. As in the case of the systems-effects of socialization, it would certainly be foolish to postpone digging into the many interesting individual-level socialization questions until the relationship between childhood states and adult states is definitively illuminated. Given such strong presumptions, it is best to proceed on all fronts simultaneously.

Political socialization is the study of political learning. It has come into prominence recently because of an increased realization that what goes on in politics is determined by people's behavior —citizens, officials, revolutionaries, diplomats, newspaper editors, image makers, and others—more than by institutional form. How the norms and consciences that undergird these behaviors are acquired has thus become a critical question.

Modern political scientists have investigated whether or not such norms and consciences may be learned while people are still of tender age. This has led to the development of an apparently new area of study, but what has really occurred is the reawakening of a venerable and prominent dimension of political theory. However, modern students of political socialization are doing more than pouring old wine in new bottles. They are focusing on empirical *evidence* and specifically asking, "Who learns what from whom under what circumstances with what effects?" Assumption, assertion, and justification of advocated programs —characteristic of the older tradition—have been replaced by investigation of what is *really* going on.

Two important kinds of concerns have developed in this new study. First is the question of the effects of political socialization.

What difference does it make for the functioning of politics that particular patterns of political socialization are present? Although these macro-level emphases are the most significant, it is unfortunately true that they are the least researched. However, there are enough suggestions of macro-level effects flowing from political socialization that we can enter this fascinating area of study with a fair degree of confidence that we are indeed engaged in a highly useful activity. Second, micro-level research focuses on explaining political socialization patterns. Why do youngsters hold the political orientations that they do?

What do children learn about politics? Do all children learn the same things? From whom do they learn? What are the processes involved in learning? These are the problems that will occupy our attention throughout this book. Of course, these micro-level questions involve some important assumptions: we must assume that childhood learning has implications for adult behavior; the evidence suggesting that this is generally the case is quite convincing. Accordingly, the study of political socialization adds up to an exciting enterprise, with immense implications for all that is political. Who holds power? Who wins elections? What policies are enacted? Who is favored? Who is discriminated against? Will revolution occur? Must political parties develop new programs? Will there be political rebellion of the younger generation? All of these questions and many more may be answered with the help of investigations in political socialization.

NOTES

1. Karl R. Popper, *The Open Society and Its Enemies,* vol. 1, 3d ed. (London: Routledge & Keagan Paul, 1957), p. 89.
2. Plato, *Republic,* trans. Francis MacDonald Cornford (New York: Oxford University Press, 1945), p. 56.
3. *Ibid.,* p. 129.
4. *Ibid.,* p. 116.
5. Carl Crow, *Master Kung* (New York: Harper and Brothers, 1938), chaps. 7, 11, 15, 16.
6. Lin Yutang, *The Wisdom of Confucius* (New York: Random House, 1943), p. 19.
7. Thomas More, *Utopia,* trans. John C. Collins (London: Clarendon Press, n.d.), p. 132.
8. Jean-Jacques Rousseau, *The Social Contract,* trans. Charles Frankel (New York: Mafner Publishing Co., 1947), p. 35; emphasis added.
9. Jean-Jacques Rousseau, "Considerations on the Government of Poland,"

in *Rousseau: Political Writings,* Frederick Watkins, ed. (London: Thomas Nelson and Sons, 1953), p. 176; emphasis added.

10. Aldous Huxley, *Brave New World* (London: Zodiac Press, 1948).
11. Nicholas DeWitt, *Education and Professional Employment in the U.S.S.R.* (Washington: National Science Foundation, 1961), p. 120.
12. Michael P. Gehlen, *The Communist Party of the Soviet Union* (Bloomington, Ind.: Indiana University Press, 1969), pp. 92–97.
13. Irene Mareuil, "Extra-Curricular and Extra-Scholastic Activities for Soviet School Children," in *The Politics of Soviet Education,* George Z. F. Bereday and Jaan Pennar, eds. (New York: Frederick A. Praeger, 1960), pp. 123–43.
14. V. I. Lenin, "The Role of Youth Leagues," in *Selected Works* (New York: International Publishers, 1943), 9; 467–82.
15. Franz L. Neumann, *Behemoth* (New York: Oxford University Press, 1942), pp. 398–99.
16. I. L. Kandel, *The Making of Nazis* (New York: Teachers' College, Columbia University, 1935), p. 17.
17. *Ibid.,* p. 42.
18. *Ibid.,* pp. 57, 85–93.
19. Neumann, *op. cit.,* pp. 428–30.
20. Werner Richter, *Re-educating Germany* (Chicago: University of Chicago Press, 1945), chap. 9.
21. W. Friedman, *The Allied Military Government of Germany* (London: Stevens and Sons, 1947), p. 180.
22. Harold Zink, *American Military Government in Germany* (New York: Macmillan Co., 1947), pp. 150–55.
23. *Ibid.,* p. 163; see also Friedman, *op. cit.,* p. 185.
24. Walter Stahl, *Education for Democracy in West Germany* (New York: Frederick A. Praeger, 1961), pp. 43–57, 83–87, 280–86.
25. Norbert Muhlen, "The Young Germans Today," *Freeman,* 28 June, 1954, pp. 705–7; Volker Bergholm, "Right-Wing Radicalism in West Germany's Younger Generation," *Journal of Central European Affairs,* 22 (October 1962): 317–36; George R. Conant, "German Textbooks and the Nazi Past," *Saturday Review,* 20 July, 1963, pp. 52–53.
26. Thomas J. Dodd, "Cold War Education: Understanding Communism Is Inadequate" (Address delivered before the Conference on Cold War Education, Tampa, Florida, 12 June, 1963), in *Vital Speeches,* 1 July, 1963, pp. 586–89; David Riesman, *Constraint and Variety in American Education* (Lincoln: University of Nebraska Press, 1956), pp. 108–21; Jack Nelson and Gene Roberts, *The Censors and the Schools* (Boston: Little Brown & Co., 1963); "Censorship of Textbooks" (Symposium), *National Education Association Journal,* 52 (May 1963): 18–26.
27. Elmer F. Pflieger and Grace L. Watson, *Emotional Adjustment: A Key to Good Citizenship* (Detroit: Wayne University Press, 1953), p. 3; William S. Vincent, *Roles of the Citizen* (Evanston, Ill: Row, Peterson Co., 1959), chap. 2; Arthur W. Foshay and Kenneth D. Wann, *Children's Social Values* (New York: Teachers' College, Columbia University, 1954), pp. 189–90.
28. Carl J. Friedrich, *Man and His Government* (New York: McGraw-Hill Book Co., 1963), pp. 619–20.
29. O. F. Raum, *Chaga Childhood: A Description of Indigenous Education in an East Africa Tribe* (New York: Oxford University Press, 1940), pp. 339–40.
30. Elizabeth A. Weber, *The Duk-Duks: Primitive and Historic Types of Citizenship* (Chicago: University of Chicago Press, 1929), pp. 1–68.

31. Kenneth L. Little, *The Mende of Sierra Leone* (New York: Oxford University Press, 1951), p. 121.
32. David Easton and Jack Dennis, *Children in the Political System* (New York: McGraw-Hill Book Co., 1969) pp. 18, 47–69.
33. Philip E. Converse and Georges Depeux, "Politicization of the Electorate in France and the United States," *Public Opinion Quarterly,* 26 (Spring 1962): 1–23.
34. Jack Dennis and Donald J. McCrone, "Preadult Development of Political Party Identification in Western Democracies," *Comparative Political Studies,* 3 (July 1970): 243–62.
35. Kenneth Prewitt and Joseph Okello-Oculi, "Political Socialization and Political Education in New Nations," in *Learning About Politics,* Roberta Sigel, ed. (New York: Random House, 1970), pp. 607–21.
36. Sidney Verba, "Conclusion: Comparative Political Culture," in *Political Culture and Political Development,* Lucien Pye and Sidney Verba, eds. (Princeton: Princeton University Press, 1965), p. 529.
37. Frederick W. Frey, "Socialization to National Identification Among Turkish Peasants," *Journal of Politics,* 30 (November 1968): 934–65.
38. David Koff and George Von Der Muhll, "Political Socialization in Kenya and Tanzania—a Comparative Analysis," *Journal of Modern African Studies,* 5 (May 1967): 13–51.
39. Gabriel Almond and Sidney Verba, *The Civic Culture* (Boston: Little, Brown & Co., 1965), esp. chaps. 5–7; Dennis and McCrone, *op. cit.,* p. 253.
40. Timothy Hennessy, "Democratic Attitudinal Configurations Among Italian Youth," *Midwest Journal of Political Science,* 13 (May 1969): 167–93.
41. Sheldon Appleton, "The Political Socialization of Taiwan's College Students," *Asian Survey,* 10 (October 1970): 910–23.
42. Fred I. Greenstein, "Political Socialization," in *International Encyclopedia of the Social Sciences,* vol. 14 (New York: Macmillan Co., 1968), pp. 552–53.
43. William A. Gamson, *Power and Discontent* (Homewood, Ill.: Dorsey Press, 1968), chap. 3; Edward S. Greenberg, "Black Children and the Political System," *Public Opinion Quarterly,* 34 (Fall 1970): 333–45.
44. Theodore M. Newcomb, "Attitude Development as a Function of Reference Groups: The Bennington Study," in *Readings in Social Psychology,* Eleanor E. Maccoby et al., eds., 3d ed. (New York: Holt, Rinehart & Winston, 1958), pp. 266–67.
45. Theodore M. Newcomb et al., *Persistence and Change: Bennington College and Its Students After Twenty-five Years* (New York: John Wiley & Sons, 1967), pp. 39–40.
46. H. A. Witkin et al., *Psychological Differentiation* (New York: John Wiley & Sons, 1962), pp. 369–70.

2. The Objects of Political Socialization: Socialization Toward What?

Chapter 1 raises more questions than it answers. Children do acquire political orientations, but what a mixed bag those orientations are. Children learn about many different kinds of political phenomena, and it behooves us to think more carefully about what these kinds are.

Most of the last chapter was—and most of this one will be— concerned with what we will call *mass socialization*. This simply refers to learning what behavior is appropriate for the citizen or subject; that is to say, behavior that may be performed by the overwhelming majority of people in a particular society, people who are amateurs in politics in the sense that they spend most of their time in nonpolitical pursuits. Being patriotic or voting are examples of mass behavior to which people are socialized.

But of course, mass behavior is not the only kind of political behavior that might interest us. The behavior of congressmen, judges, policemen, military officers, and revolutionaries is also a legitimate concern of the student of politics. The study of such figures has been prominent in political science. How do people acquire the dispositions to perform the behavior suited for these roles? Here, too, the answer must be in part through socialization. It is quite possible that youthful experience may predispose an individual to become, say, a legislator or party leader. We shall call the acquisition of such orientations *elite socialization*.[1]

MASS SOCIALIZATION

It is likely that most very young children, say, under the age of two, believe their parents to be virtually omnipotent. Parents, after all, do control most aspects of the life of the very young. Most of a child's crucial needs, like food supply and affection, as well as basic family behavior patterns (bedtimes, outings, and so on), appear to be dispensed or regulated by parents. Psychologists suggest that, as a result, much of the world must seem to conform to the will of the parent. It is not at all uncommon for children, in full expectation of being satisfied, to ask parents to make it stop raining, to produce lost toys, or to conjure up specific desired television shows at any time.

However, it is only a matter of time before the child's world expands sufficiently so that he can no longer realistically believe his parents to be the prime movers of the world. In general, the child soon becomes aware of two kinds of limitations on parental power. Natural phenomena proceed independently of parental desires. Picnics get rained out, snow prevents a trip. New super-powers enter the child's cognitive field—powers attributed to nature or God. However, a second disillusionment is inevitable. Not only are parents soon seen as subject to natural or religious authority, but to *social authority* as well. Man-made restrictions such as traffic laws constrain parents; children quickly learn this. Authority figures such as police become visible.[2] Again, the formerly (perceived to be) omnipotent parents bend, this time to the will of other men or the institutions of men. The new superpowers are political authority.

Thus, cognitively at least, children begin while they are relatively young to undergo political socialization. It is likely that affective socialization accompanies the cognitive, for in general, children's awareness of new authorities is accompanied by some evaluative criteria. It is easy to believe that children are curious about the moral qualities of such potent agents and demand evaluations of them from parents. Further, it takes no great study of political and religious history to know that there has been no dearth of people anxious to provide youngsters with moral evaluations of these agents. Probably, children are initially urged to regard religious and political superpowers positively, as kind, benevolent, and serving. Few modern cultures transmit images of capriciousness or danger in connection with such agents. Older generations try to reassure children rather than to increase their anxiety.

Furthermore, some scholars think that the original awareness of political authority is indeed momentous, one of the dramatic experiences of young life. According to these writers, political authority may have great anxiety potential. The child becomes aware of a tremendously powerful agent. How can it be propitiated? In order to avoid the totally debilitating anxiety that would accompany entertaining doubts or uncertainties about the moral character of this superpower (its destructive capabilities must be enormous, for political authority clearly is superior even to the once all-powerful parents), youngsters *must* regard political authority as kind, benevolent, and good.[3] Affective socialization, according to this argument, proceeds as a necessary consequence of cognitive socialization.

Regardless of whether or not this is a good argument, it is clear that the very young do undergo political socialization. Indeed, the first prominent finding of the new research on political socialization was that American children not only become aware of the President, a prominent and visible political authority figure, but come to view him in extremely idealized, positive terms. He is seen, indeed, as a benevolent leader.[4]

However, this is only a beginning. What else do children come to know and believe? What other political objects besides the President cross their vision? In fact, there are quite a number of objects, with many different implications. The picture is not a simple one. (Indeed, it may even be that high positive regard for the President is not universal.) Children are socialized to a diverse, and sometimes confusing, set of objects.

We can explore this problem by adopting Easton's classification of political objects.[5] We can classify citizens' political orientations as being directed toward one of three kinds of political phenomena: the community, the regime, or the government. Community may be thought of as roughly equivalent to *nation*. More generally, Easton and Dennis argue that community refers to a collection of persons who share a division of political labor.

> Part of what uniquely identifies a member of the French political system, for example, is his belief that there are others with whom he should participate in making and implementing most day-to-day decisions and whom he calls his fellow Frenchmen or countrymen. It does not matter that in fact he is totally uninvolved in politics and cooperates with the other members of the system only to the extent that he complies with political outputs. He shares a political community with others in that he does not expect that these daily political issues will be resolved through a structure that will normally include, say, those in Germany or Great Britain.[6]

Words used to describe *support* for the political community on the part of the mass citizenry are *patriotism* and *nationalism*. Of course, throughout history, much political socialization has been directed at this goal. Mass emotional commitment to the homeland has been asked and gladly made in the name of the nation during all the great wars of the nineteenth and twentieth centuries, as well as all the recent independence movements. It is clear that socialization to support of the community is a powerful weapon for the maintenance or construction of political systems, and it is clear that socialization to lack of support for the community is highly desirable for revolutionaries and iconoclasts.

Nonsupport for the political community could be demonstrated in a variety of ways; it could be shown by almost any kind of political nonconformity. But perhaps the most obvious types of behavior would be separatism and emigration. The current French separatist movement in Quebec is clearly community-level behavior. No doubt, Canadian officials are wondering how the Quebec separatists were socialized to their anticommunity beliefs. The American Civil War involved the integrity of the political community, as did the Revolutionary War, which created the American political community and modified the British.

All these events depended heavily on mass behavior, and the political orientations on which they were based may well have been the product of political socialization.

Regime may roughly be thought of as the community's "rules of the game," the constitutional order, or the structure of authority. Scholars are wont to talk about different types of regimes, using terms like *monarchy, aristocracy,* or *democracy* to describe arrangements that indicate how decisions are made in the political arena. Adoption of new constitutions and most revolutions (e.g., French and Russian) represent regime-level changes within political communities. Sometimes the word *patriotism* is also used to describe mass support for the regime. Surely most Americans would tend to think of anyone who advocated overthrow of the Constitution of 1789 as unpatriotic. Indeed, Americans are unlikely to make a differentiation between support for the political community (United States) and support for the political regime (present constitutional arrangement). However, it should be clear that the two are logically separable. The framers of the 1789 Constitution could be said to have perpetrated a revolution against the regime by overthrowing the Articles of Confederation, but they claimed to do so in the name of supporting the community, asserting that only if the regime were changed could the community survive. Similarly, it appears that the French support regimes only weakly—they change "republics" rather frequently, and there are still citizens who would like to restore the monarchy. Yet, the French are supposedly among the most patriotic people in the world—from the standpoint of the community, *la belle France.*

Of course, whether citizens support the existing arrangements or reject them in favor of revolution and a new regime is indeed a key question. As noted in chapter 1, all regimes have sought to prevent erosions in their own mass support through developing programs of political socialization, while all would-be usurpers of power have no doubt pondered whether their own countersocialization efforts were more efficacious than those of the establishment.

Government, as an object of socialization, is best appreciated by invoking the sense in which the British use that word. They speak of a Labour government or of a Conservative government to indicate which party controls the policy-making organs of the regime. Government, as an object of socialization, consists not of the formal institutions and offices involved in making policy, but of the specific persons who hold these offices and the particular policies they enact. In the American Presidential system, the analogue would be the term *administration,* prefaced by the name of the President in office. Government-level socialization refers to questions about policy and policy makers, about political phenomena that take place on a regular basis within a political system. Support or lack of support for an incumbent President, loyalty to a political party, opposition to a change in the draft laws, all constitute mass orientations at the government level. All are presumably products of political socialization. Government-level political behavior may be the type Americans think of most often. Elections are perhaps the most visible political phenomena in the U.S., and much attention is focused on them. Responding to this government-level interest, public opinion polls frequently "predict" electoral outcomes. Similarly, we wonder whether public officials are maintaining their popularity, and opinion pollsters oblige with monthly surveys of the public. We are interested in whether a "majority" favors legalizing "pot" or whether citizens are coming to favor effective control of environmental pollution. How many favor pulling out of Vietnam? How many favor escalating the war?

Perhaps we are most conscious of these government-level considerations because *controversy* surrounds them as a matter of course. Indeed, although politics is basically a process by which conflicts between people are resolved, disputes are much more common at this level. In the United States, contemporary unrest and violence notwithstanding, community or regime conflict has been rare, while government-level controversy has, of course, been rife. Most people agree that the community of the United States ought to exist (at least there is relatively little demand for merging it with some other political entity or subdividing it into smaller political communities) and that the regime defined by the 1789 Constitution and subsequent decisions and documents ought not to undergo extensive and rapid change. In fact, most do not think of such questions as political at all. People who raise them are even regarded as traitorous, participants in crime rather than in politics. Americans have lived in a relatively placid country in relatively placid times. But Presidents, parties, and policies are accepted as fit topics for argumentation.

Children, of course, become socialized about things like party conflict. And such matters are important and deserve to be studied.

But it is important to know something about the sources of the orientations that *most people share,* as well as those which conflict with each other.

Of course, the three-fold classification of political socialization objects—community-regime-government—is not perfectly or completely unambiguous. Suppose someone desires a Constitutional amendment to make prayers in the public schools a part of the regular curriculum. Essentially, this is a policy matter (government level), but yet the Constitutional order (regime level) is undergoing modification. Similarly, suppose we come upon a situation where a city is seeking to annex surrounding areas, or where consolidated urban government is being proposed for an area consisting of a central city and numerous suburbs. No doubt considerable controversy would erupt about the continuance of some political units and the creation of new ones. People will differ as to which jurisdiction they wish to live under. Is this an example of community-level conflict? It is clearly quite different from that surrounding the integrity of a nation-state, but, given American local government, it does involve political specialization of labor. Despite these problems, however, the community-regime-government scheme does serve as a useful tool for thinking. As we shall see, it is particularly appropriate for dealing with the questions of mass political socialization.

Community-Level Socialization. Perhaps the most important step in the intellectual development of human beings is the ability to distinguish between different classes or categories of objects. All persons, beginning when they are children, develop some facility in this regard. Most significant of the distinctions one learns to draw are those between the "self" and "others." Self-other distinctions can take many forms. Individuals come to see themselves as members of many classes or groups which are somehow set off from other classes or groups. Children come to know quite early that they are, for example, boys rather than girls, blacks rather than whites, poor rather than rich, or Protestant rather than Catholic or Jewish. By the time an American child is about six years old, a self-other distinction involving his membership in the political community United States has joined the rapidly lengthening list.[7]

Probably more interesting than children's recognition of the political community is the way in which they come to evaluate it. A typical pattern in the United States (and there is much evidence that this is true elsewhere as well) is for development of positive emotions for the entity "America." [8] The precise way in which this predisposition (or, for that matter, its atypical opposite) comes about is not altogether clear. It is known that children do develop very positive feelings toward objects that are local and close. Objects that are proximate are meaningful, and, everything else being equal, these are the objects that will be loved and cherished. Of course, few of the salient objects within the purview of the young child are at all political in nature. Typically, youngsters think highly of their pets, their friends, the trees they see, their house, the music they hear. No other pets, friends, and so on, could possibly match those that they know. [9] But these attachments appear to have political payoffs. The very young associate their immediate surroundings with the nation. They claim to love their country *because* of the beauty of the trees, the (perceived) quality of the weather, the friendliness of their associates, or other equally mundane reasons. It appears, then, that some sort of *generalization* from familiar and loved surroundings to the more abstract notion of the political community takes place.

Of course, there are a few objects in the immediate life of the young child that have more explicit linkages to the political community. These are national symbols, particularly national flags. Several studies have demonstrated that children come early to prefer the flag of their own country. Moreover, it is clear that this preference has nothing to do with aesthetic considerations of pattern, color, or proportion. It appears to be invested with emotional attachment to the nation. Given the fact that the connection of the flag to the nation is frequently and ceremoniously made in school and elsewhere, it is not at all difficult to think that children generalize feelings about this familiar object to the political community. [10]

It is also possible that community-level affective socialization is partly an unanticipated consequence of religious teachings. Children are typically taught that religious authority is benevolent and loving, both at home and as part of more formal church activities. If, as already suggested, children's early relationships to political authority are similar to their orientations to religious authority, it may be that some of the positive feelings toward religion are extended to political figures as well. There is some evidence that young children confuse religious ritual with patriotic observance. The similarity between hymns and national anthems, between flags and crosses, is obvious. Great sanctity can surround both realms. It is not at all surprising that U.S. children regard the pledge of allegiance as a prayer, as indeed a request to God for aid and protection.[11]

A few scholars have tried to explore community-level socialization beyond these very basic findings. One area of study has dealt with the extent to which children think in terms of narrow, personalistic interests, on the one hand, or in terms of collective interests—those shared by many people—on the other. Two key questions have emerged from this. The first has to do with the extent that children can think of subordinating their own or some other individual's interest to some *community* of interest, with implications for collective benefit. It is the old question of private interest versus public interest. No doubt the prominent belief that it is *better* to be oriented to public interest than private is in part responsible for the interest in this kind of research. A second major question concerns the extent to which children are capable of thinking in terms of some international community rather than a community corresponding to one nation. Again, it is a "narrow, selfish" as opposed to "broad, enlightened" kind of dichotomy. Unquestionably, this concern stems from an interest in lessening international tensions and avoiding international conflict. Its underlying moral principle is probably that nationalism is bad and ought to be eliminated.

These two parallel "narrow-broad" questions have been attacked from the standpoint of cognitive development. At what age are children sufficiently sophisticated to grasp the idea of community, as opposed to personal interest (or international, as opposed to national)? This bears similarity to a problem that has been an obsession with educators. At what age are children "ready to learn" certain concepts?

It should come as no great surprise that, until perhaps the mid-teens, children think of the political system as a device for

serving personal ends. But at about this time, views begin to
change about the obligations of living in a political community,
e.g., submission to compulsory vaccination laws or payment of
taxes. The great majority of eleven-year-olds see vaccination as a
device for protection of individual health, but their counterparts
at the age of eighteen think of it as necessary for community survival.[12] Another way of putting this is to say that younger children think of the political community as a device for restraining
people from indulging destructive impulses. They must be pre-
vented from hurting themselves or others. On the other hand,
older youths see that political organization can be used to improve the human condition and is necessary for the achievement of
goals that are individually impossible to obtain.[13] Coupled with
other findings (e.g., with age comes less emphasis on the necessity
of political coercion and the emphasis on restraint declines), these
results may be regarded as encouraging. Dissolution of society
into privatism may seem unlikely. But from another perspective,
these findings, though interesting, are quite inadequate. We do
not know what causes people to be public-interest oriented and
we do not know much about the relationship between this kind
of thinking and affect. Do public-interested people love their
political community?

At best, the work on cognitive development suggests when certain kinds of political orientations are *possible*. It has little ability
to predict different levels of affect toward the political community,
nor does it suggest the sources of different levels of development.
Is it a matter of actual physiological maturation of the brain,
differential exposure to teaching, or still other influences? In point
of fact, these findings lead us little further than the descriptions
of basic orientations to the community.

But efforts are being made to understand the central questions
of national loyalty. Significantly, some concern is being devoted to
race. It is reasonable to suppose that blacks in the United States
would be less positively committed to the political community
than whites. One hears occasional demands for "black separatism," the establishment of an independent black nation carved
out of the present territory of the United States. If socialization to
the political community is important, we would expect some of

these black-white differences to be revealed in children. Black and white children in grades three to nine were asked whether they agreed or disagreed with a statement about pride in being an American and were instructed to select the "best" flag from among several, including the American. Black children were indeed slightly less enthusiastic about America.[14] But two other interesting results also emerged. The differences between white and black children increased with age; though at third grade level racial differences were minimal, the ninth grade differential was more substantial. This suggests that the factors accounting for relatively low black affect may operate most strongly in later childhood and even grow in importance during adolescence or young adulthood. Among these factors, it is reasonable to suppose, is awareness of racial discrimination in the United States. It is known that black children who perceive racial inequities are less likely to support the political community, and it is probable that such awareness, in fact, increases with age. Thus, it is possible that knowledge of racial discrimination among blacks translates directly into lessened community-level support. As black youngsters become old enough to acquire this knowledge, their withdrawal seems likely.

In general, three things can be said of political socialization to the political community. First, undoubtedly very young children do come to have some ideas about their nation. Typically, they express very positive attitudes that may be the result of generalizing from other experiences. Second, it is clear that the level of cognitive development (which is associated with age) determines that certain conceptions of the public or national interest are possible at different stages. Third, there is growing concern with the need to account for community-level socialization. Why do some people support it and some not? This latter problem is clearly very important. The example of racial differences is just one of many that can easily be imagined. Emigrant groups might be investigated, as might "revolutionary" protest groups. We can look forward to more information in this third area, for it is here that most interest lies and here that research will be done.

Regime-Level Socialization. Although regime and community are conceptually distinct, they may not always be so empirically.

This is true not only because citizens may be unable to disentangle beliefs and feelings they have toward these objects, but also because community-level socialization and regime-level socialization may be related and have effects on each other. If a regime is popular, and enjoys great support, people may come to associate it with the community—much as youngsters come to associate pleasant items in their immediate surroundings with the community. Similarly, a despised regime may be thought so onerous that everything associated with it—including the community—may lose support. It is clear that many leaders in the United States South tried to institute regime-level changes in the 1850's to allow for greater autonomy—they clearly did not support the then-current regime. But as regime-level changes were not forthcoming, nonsupport spread to the community with quite drastic results. In short, regime-level support can become an important ingredient in community-level support.

Two distinct kinds of regime-level socialization deserve our attention. The first has to do with children's responses to the symbols and institutions of the regime. This is very straightforward. The key questions are, What regime phenomena do children perceive and what do they think about them? Do they love the President, the Constitution, and so on, or do they not? The second has to do with behavioral norms. Some kinds of behavior are appropriate to a particular kind of regime. For example, in an absolute monarchy, the mass population might consider themselves to be subjects rather than citizens; they would tend to be passive and believe themselves incapable of judging the wisdom or unwisdom of various public policies. If, for some reason, these norms began to change, the persistence of a monarchical regime might be in grave doubt. In fact, the decline of monarchy throughout the world over the last several centuries has often been attributed to mass changes in norms about the proper role of citizens. Whether norms and beliefs are congruent with regimes is a matter of great significance.

The first regime symbols or institutions of which the American child becomes aware are the President and the policeman. The prominence of the President and the attention given him in the mass media, as well as in children's literature, makes him a prime candidate for a central role in youthful conceptions of political affairs. The policeman's prominence is due to his high visibility—nearly all children can identify him as a figure of public order simply because he is a familiar person who occupies a portion of the child's direct attention. By the second grade, youngsters are clearly aware of these two political officers.

More significant than mere awareness is evaluation. Much research has shown that the very young typically have an exaggerated, highly positive image of the President. He is seen as standing at the apex of the political hierarchy, with all other public officials in clearly subordinate positions and acting only at Presidential command. But not only is he superpowerful, but he is also seen to be superbenevolent. However, this image becomes somewhat tarnished as children mature. They become less inclined to impute superlative qualities to the chief executive, and are more inclined to value his role-filling capacities (energy, intelligence) than his personal qualities (kindliness, morality). This obviously indicates increasing realism and ability to differentiate between political roles. Similarly, the maturing child becomes more aware of other governmental institutions, and these come to be positively regarded at the expense of the previously all-powerful and benign President. Congress, especially, emerges as a favored institution, as does the law.

These data suggest that the figure of the President plays an important role in the introduction of the young to politics. There are two particularly fascinating questions raised by this. First, is it necessary for the young and unsophisticated to *personify* authority? Must the young mind, capable of only limited understanding, search out a human figure to which great capacity is attached and toward whom love is expressed? This is not a new idea by any means. Bagehot, commenting on government in Britain in the nineteenth century, suggested that a personal authority figure was necessary to perform a symbolic function for the ignorant and credulous masses. The king was the object that could be loved and respected—the more abstract notion of Parliament and ministers could not inspire such loyalty. If Presidents, in a parallel fashion, provide a symbol for the young to respect, they may indeed be extremely important in the establishment of regime-level support. But what happens in nations where there is no readily available authority figure to act as symbol? The Soviet Union, for example, has divided executive responsibility *and* a historical figure—Lenin—who may serve as an authority symbol. Nor, perhaps, is there a single authority symbol in France. Indeed, there is evidence that French children are more likely to impute bad (29 per cent) rather than good (24 per cent) qualities to the president of the republic.[15]

The second question is raised time and again in discussions of childhood political socialization. Are these youthful political orientations related to later attitudes and behavior on the part of adults? We know that the positive Presidential image does not persist as such into adulthood—adults are really quite cynical about executive figures—but many scholars believe that there are important payoffs in adult regime support. However, a caveat is in order. Some of the data revealing that children typically hold a positive image of the President were collected in the late 1950's and early 1960's. The picture of highly consensual regime support that they present may contrast somewhat with highly visible political dissent by college-age youth in the 1970's. This is especially noteworthy, because the age groups interviewed in the 1950's are now the age groups in college from whom the protests are heard. The childhood data gave no hint of future regime-level protest. It is possible that *later* experiences are behind such behavior, and not youthful Presidential images at all.

Though it is possible that early views of the President are meaningless for later authority orientations, it would be foolish to jump to this conclusion immediately. Some data on respect for the policeman, the other prominent authority figure for children, bear on this point. Although the typical childhood reaction to the policeman is *similar* to that to the President (high regard, especially on dimensions of helpfulness, which declines slightly with age), it cannot be said that the policeman is an object of idealization. Children are more realistic about him, no doubt, because of his proximity. However, the high regard in which he is typically held is—as for the President—often interpreted to translate into later regime support. "If as children matured they came to despise, distrust, scorn, or reject the police, the probabilities would be considerable . . . that acceptance of the whole structure of authority at all levels would suffer." [16]

One can make a slightly better judgment about this statement than the parallel one about the President. For one thing, there is evidence that the child's image of the policeman is not so universally favorable.[17] We can look at groups in the population who appear to be least regime supportive and ask whether children in these groups are less favorable toward police. As a group, blacks surely have been involved in considerable political protest, and some of it has been aimed (according to leaders) specifically at the regime. If this lack of enthusiasm for the regime has childhood roots, one would expect today's black children to be more hostile toward police than their white counterparts. Recent studies show that this is, in fact, the case. On several dimensions, like honesty, fairness, and objectivity of the police, ninth to twelfth grade blacks were considerably more questioning.[18] A similar investigation showed that while third grade blacks were willing to assert that policemen were friendly, helpful, and likable, the proportion dropped precipitously with age. Fifth-, seventh-, and ninth-graders had no such image of the policeman.[19] It is interesting to speculate on the long-term implications of such findings—especially when we note that this negativism is concentrated among children who accurately perceive that blacks are not accorded equal opportunity in this country.

Another approach to the meaning of youthful orientations to authority figures also involves studies of police. Instead of regarding affect toward President or policemen as in itself an indication of regime support, a recent report considered that the ultimate in that support was *willingness to comply with the laws*. This makes good sense, for a regime in which authority figures were idealized but in which no one obeyed the laws would be in deep trouble, indeed. The critical question then becomes, Does affect for the policeman in any way contribute to compliance? For white children, at least, this appears to be the case.[20] Those who hold the policeman in high regard are compliant; those who do not are less compliant. If this pattern is maintained over the years, police orientation could be a significant precursor of regime support.

In short, there is some evidence (although it is by no means complete) that youthful images of authority figures do have some relationship to the support given to the regime.

On the regime level, the problem of fostering *particular norms and beliefs* has generated at least as much controversy as the question of support for symbols, figures, and institutions. In our culture, interest has centered on "democratic" norms or their absence. As noted in chapter 1, the realization has been profound that governmental forms cannot be ensured through specified manipulation of institution or written constitution. Instead of asking what kind of institutional practice makes democracy workable, intellectuals now ask whether the masses are likely to make good democratic citizens. Not surprisingly, the key democratic norms are supposed to encompass tolerance and openness on the one hand and political participation on the other.

Tolerance—or its absence—has received considerable attention in recent years. Studies of American adults have revealed interesting and surprising findings. Though many people profess support of the Declaration of Independence or the Bill of Rights, they are, perhaps, responding to patriotic symbols only, for the same individuals sometimes reject the specific principles of those documents in actual application. This kind of evidence, plus the fact that clearly antidemocratic dictators and demagogues occasionally find widespread mass support even in supposedly democratic nations, cannot but be of concern to the student of political socialization. How do people come to be politically tolerant—or intolerant? Are they socialized to either a democratic or authoritarian character while young? Is it a result of early acquired levels of general dogmatism?

Widespread democratic political participation is thought to be vitally important nearly everywhere in the world. According to most democratic theory, widespread participation means responsive government, maximally gratifying policies, and, consequently, greatest citizen contentment. Failure to participate means that minority rule—less generally satisfying and perhaps pernicious—occurs by default. Alternately, democratic theory teaches that widespread mass participation makes great collective accomplishment possible. Only through citizen involvement can governments pursue technological or human development programs—or resist aggression from other nations. Accordingly, the question of how to motivate a perhaps ignorant and indolent citizenry to the necessary action receives high priority. In the democratic West, the exhortation to vote is heard at every election time; people are expected to exercise the franchise as part of a solemn duty. A similar note is prominent in the developing nations of the world, where new regimes cope with the problem of how to make participatory citizens out of persons whose tribal heritages provide little relevant experience. In either case, perhaps the necessary motivation springs from feeling "efficacious" politically, that is, the belief that participation has a meaningful impact on government. Possibly, a sense of citizen duty—an obligation to participate—is similarly critical.

The search for possible childhood roots of these and similar norms has been interesting. It is clear that the idea of participation—and especially the idea of exerting *influence* on government—develops much later in children than affect toward regime symbols. In fact, it is not unreasonable to argue that the "benevolent leader" image that children have of Presidents and other figures could lead to a "subject" or passive, as opposed to "citizen" or active, orientation—with consequences for the way government authority is viewed. In the very early grades, children do typically express belief in "rule by the people," but this appears to be a response only on the verbal level. Youngsters cannot articulate what "rule by the people" means. They have no idea that they might work their will on government officials. The third or fourth grade child considers the role of citizen to involve neatness, orderliness, obedience, and avoidance of any kind of antisocial behavior. This conception of the citizen—which is certainly promoted and encouraged by the curriculums and conduct of most elementary schools—gives way by seventh or eighth grade to a conception with some participatory emphases.[21] Although these participatory dimensions may be considered quite narrowly—perhaps with an almost exclusive emphasis on voting—they become more prominent with age, as does increasing willingness to accept diverse points of view.[22] The fact that the typical fifteen-year-old in Western nations is more democratic in his orientations than the typical ten-year-old is, for many observers, a source of great encouragement.

Do these early orientations have any implications for the holding of regime-level norms by adult populations? Again, there is no obvious and conclusive answer to this critical question, but there is considerable evidence of a strong connection. Referring once more to the racial situation in the United States, it is reasonable to think that American blacks are less enthusiastic than whites about participating in the American political system, less likely to believe that government activity is meaningful or salient, and less likely than whites to believe that they can have an impact on government. If this very important regime-level orientation has childhood roots, we would expect black children to manifest fewer feelings of political efficacy than their white counterparts. Indeed, they do just that. In one survey, at every grade level from fifth to twelfth, black youngsters were more inclined to agree with statements like the following: "What happens in the government will happen no matter what people do. It is like the weather, there is nothing people can do about it." "There are some big, powerful men in the government who are running the whole thing and they do not care about us ordinary people." [23] Though it would clearly be inadequate to say that a nonparticipatory minority is being created during childhood, the significance of findings like this should not be underestimated.

A similar finding—which should cause consternation to women's lib advocates—has to do with sex differences. There is no question that in the United States women are less politically active, are less participatory than men. They vote less, join fewer organizations, do less party work, read less, and care less about politics. Moreover, contrary to many persons' beliefs, this does not, in general, stem from restrictions imposed on women—e.g., being tied to the home by responsibility for children. It results in large part from a set of norms that women hold: that they should not be as participatory as men, that politics is a man's game. Are women socialized to these nonparticipatory orientations as children? If they are, girls ought to differ from boys on such dimensions at very early ages. On most measurements they do, with girls decidedly less political. Girls are less oriented to various kinds of political action and are decidedly less informed. Moreover, these sexual differences are evident as early as fourth grade. Despite increased efforts to involve women in the political world, despite all the recent attention, there is a cultural tradition of feminine nonparticipation transmitted in childhood. "Aspects of children's political development . . . make it clear that political sex differences . . . are unlikely to vanish soon." [24]

Finally, there are some cross-national comparative data revealing that youth fall into a pattern that might be predicted on the basis of adult cultures. Some nations clearly have less democratic traditions than others. This is true even among relatively "advanced" nations of European heritage. Undoubtedly, the most discussed and most puzzling departure from democratic traditions has been twentieth-century Germany. The whole Nazi experience seems to indicate that the degree of commitment to democratic ideals has been generally quite weak in that country. Other evidence reinforces the notion of lack of personal flexibility and of deference to established authority in many areas of life. Continuing concern about the re-emergence of Nazism (among both Germans and non-Germans) shows that this is a widespread fear. Popular discussion has it that these features spring from early experience with a typically German authoritarian and father-dominated family. Although a full test of this hypothesis would be difficult to perform, we can investigate the question of whether such orientations seem to have childhood roots by comparing German youngsters with those from countries whose democratic traditions are less fragile. If the former exhibited fewer or weaker democratic norms, we would be more inclined to guess that children's regime-level orientations persist into adulthood and contribute to the dominant culture. A recent investigation of nine- to fifteen-year-old schoolchildren in four countries revealed exactly such parallels. On political-efficacy points, like those already discussed, Germans were notably less democratic than their counterparts elsewhere. "The United States is highest, Britain second, Italy third, and Germany lowest at every age level." [25] A similar difference was revealed on questions having to do with tolerance of minorities or of criticism of the government. "The political socialization of German children to tolerance of dissent is not assured." [26]

Of course, these data cannot be interpreted to mean that democracy in Germany is impossible or that German adults are in some fundamental way antidemocratic (indeed, recent public opinion poll data show increasing support for democratic norms), but the authors of this study felt that German youth may hold their democratic commitments "more lightly." This, of course, is congruent with observations of adult German culture.

Thus, it is clear that, typically, considerable regime-level socialization occurs during childhood. Early positive evaluations of authority figures become considerably more realistic as the child grows older, but, despite the decline, there is evidence that these images may be related to adult attachment to the symbols and figures of the regime and thus to support for the regime.

The democratic regime-level norms of influence through participation and of tolerance of diverse political views emerge somewhat later than overt regime support—perhaps not until thirteen years of age or so—but they appear to grow in importance through childhood. Although the question is by no means settled, there is much evidence that childhood orientations on this dimension persist into adulthood. Taking all of the evidence together, it is a reasonable, if tentative, conclusion that what children learn while still quite young is very important to the probability that given regimes will persist and to the character of these regimes.

Government-Level Socialization. Clearly, the most prevalent kind of mass behavior at the government level—at least in Western democracies—is voting. Of course, government-level behavior can involve more than this. Merely holding an opinion about an issue or a candidate can constitute significant behavior. Distributions of opinions—revealed in polls, constituent mail, or informal conversation—could govern the behavior of convention delegates, members of Congress, bureaucrats, or other elites. Simple membership in organizations that try to influence the policy process may have a similar effect, for the sheer size of a pressure group can influence its effectiveness.

Moreover, much government-level behavior—for example, that of the leaders of interest groups—is, of course, not mass behavior at all. Elites perform many acts that have a direct bearing on government activity and public policy—some would say a more direct impact than mass behavior has.

Because voting is a prominent government-level behavior, a

good way of classifying children's government-level orientations is that suggested by the concepts which the University of Michigan's Survey Research Center uses to analyze adult voting. These are: candidate orientation, issue orientation, and party identification.[27] These are very simple notions. A voting decision may rest on an assessment of a candidate's personal qualities, some judgment about issues raised in the campaign, permanent loyalty to party, or some combination of these. Most citizens apparently use these three factors in structuring much of what they see at the government level of political phenomena. It behooves us to examine the possibility of childhood precursors of each.

Knowing what we do about children's tendency to hold a highly positive image of the President, it should come as no surprise that youngsters, from the most tender age, evaluate candidates. Not surprisingly, at the beginning, *all* candidates are evaluated highly favorably. There appears to be great reluctance to perceive any public figure unfavorably.[28] Parallel to this, children —even up to and beyond eighth grade—believe that conflict and disagreement between candidates is a bad thing. Everybody should be working for the common good. This fundamental failure to understand that government is a social-conflict settling device is repeated in judgments about parties.[29] No doubt, this curious tendency is responsible for the great misunderstanding about political conflict, which is easy to see all around us. A legacy of the early milk-and-honey image of candidate relationships may well be cynicism when it confronts harsh reality. Despite this, children can and do articulate candidate preferences in elections. They do make distinctions; they do care.

There may be an interesting by-product of overly positive candidate orientations. In some political systems, government-level orientations may be held so strongly that there is "spill-over" to the regime level. The supporters of a losing candidate may regard the defeat as so monumental, may find the hated winner so distasteful, that they perpetrate revolution to prevent him from coming to office. Government-level defeat, because the differences at this level are felt so strongly, triggers rejection of the regime. Latin American examples are not hard to come by. There is no hint of spill-over in American children. Indeed, when faced with the fact that a preferred candidate has lost an election, children in the lower grades again refer to their conception of politics as conflictless. The defeated candidate should help the winner to govern successfully and beneficially. The winner is also highly regarded; a positive image is built up of him as well.[30] From the standpoint of regime survival, it is impressive that this pattern should exist in a nation that has a history of stability of regime. The congruence between children's orientations and what we observe to be characteristic of long-term adult behavior suggests that the effects of childhood socialization regarding candidate orientations do persist to meaningfully affect political life.

Of course, as children mature and critical capacities develop, this primitive candidate orientation changes somewhat. Exposure to political reality has some effect. More refined candidate orientation develops; negative evaluations are possible. Other criteria for judgment—perhaps even public-policy-related ones—come into play. However, given the frequency with which adults seem to base their candidate preferences on speech, dress, appearance, or features of personal life, one cannot but wonder exactly how much development takes place from the primitive state.

Given the early, conflictless image of politics, it is not surprising that children really have little, if any, notion of issues until at least eighth grade. Indeed, even at that age only 6 per cent are able to make issue distinctions between parties, and a typical comment of those 6 per cent would be, "The Republicans are for the rich people." [31] A full half of the adult population can reach this modest level of sophistication. The great differences between adults and eighth-graders suggest considerable development during the high school years. Indeed, other evidence suggests that high school seniors have acquired considerable capacity for assuming different positions on issues.[32] It must be said, however, that, by the time children are in sixth grade, the idea of inducing change through public policy is common.[33] They understand that laws can be modified, that human will can be implemented through government action. But, in general, they do not envisage *disputes* over these matters. The sixth-grader appears to think that collective goals can be pursued by political acclamation. Contentious *issues* are yet invisible. During the grade school years, political policy is understandable, though apparently political conflict is not.

Although it is certainly reasonable to interpret this limited attention to issues as a consequence of intellectual underdevelopment, a condition likely to change with maturation and the growth of mental capacities, it is also interesting to note that the American adult public is notoriously ignorant of issues. Perhaps the parallel between children and adults is a significant one.

The remaining feature of government-level orientation, party identification, proves to be extremely widespread in American children. As the previous few paragraphs would lead one to guess, this orientation has little substantive implication for the child, although he is aware that party symbols differentiate political objects. Moreover, even as early as fourth grade, as many as 60 per cent of the children themselves claim allegiance to one or the other of the major parties, a figure that increases with age. Indeed, even in *second* grade, only a third of the children are unable to attach meaning to the names of the parties.[34] Again, this pattern bears a striking congruence to what we know about party life in America. The two major parties have jointly enjoyed an unbroken hegemony over a very long period of time. The party system has been supported generation after generation. Probably related to this is the fact that the overwhelming majority of American adults hold party identification to some degree. The early transmission of party identification to children may be an essential part of the continuance of this process.

Even more suggestive of the persistence and importance of youthful partisanship are some comparative data. Children in many Western democratic nations show a similar development of partisan identification with age. However, the rate and extent of development varies from country to country. The most partisan youth are found in Great Britain and the United States, exactly those countries that have the greatest proportion of partisan adults *and* the oldest and most stable party systems. On the other hand, in France, even among late adolescents, only a bare majority can be mustered who are party-identified—and it is France, of course, that has the most conspicuous history of party instability.[35]

Thus, there is no question that children do acquire government-level political orientations on each of the three dimensions: candidate orientation, issue orientation, and party identification. Once again, although we cannot say with any degree of certainty that childhood learning determines adult politics, we cannot ignore the extent to which children's orientations correspond to known adult behavior patterns or to the characteristics of political systems that we can observe on an everyday basis. Put another way, there is no sound basis for rejecting the idea that childhood government-level socialization is important.

ELITE SOCIALIZATION

To be sure, the socialization of elites is a very different process from the socialization of masses. For one thing, relevant political behavior on the part of elites—leadership, policy decision making—is not performed by the masses. In addition, the mix of child and adult socialization may be quite different. While it is likely that much of the basis for mass behavior is learned during the early years, it is reasonable to think that considerable learning about elite positions—say that of a city councilman—cannot be acquired until the individual actually occupies the position. In the United States, people are rarely trained specifically for public office, and they may have to wait until they are actually installed before much necessary learning can take place. Many other interesting questions about elite socialization come readily to mind. For example, in some countries there is a relatively conscious effort to develop political leaders, starting at a young age. Great Britain's educational system prepares a pool of elite expertise from which most political leaders will be drawn. What are the implications for political life of different elite socialization patterns?

Although the combinations of different kinds of experiences may differ between elites and mass and among elites in different cultures, there is considerable evidence that childhood events may be important in the subsequent lives of political leaders. Biographies of a number of political figures are studded with descriptions of dramatic events in childhood that supposedly had lasting and significant impact and which thus account for some success (or failure). The dominating, uncompromising political style of Woodrow Wilson (which may have figured heavily in his failure to bring the United States into the League of Nations) is asserted to be a reaction to the damaged self-esteem he suffered as a child at the hands of a demanding and ridiculing father.[36] Lenin's dramatic political behavior—that of playing a key role in one of the major revolutions in history—supposedly depended in part upon his adolescent experiences. While Lenin was a teen-ager, his brother was hanged for allegedly participating in a plot to assassinate the Czar. Lenin, who witnessed the event, never lost his determined revolutionary fervor.[37] Lesser figures are also thought to have made their peculiar contributions to history because of some juvenile or adolescent experiences. James Forrestal, a post-World War II secretary of defense, is a particularly good example. Forrestal's impact on American foreign policy during that period was considerable. He was one of the first officials to emphasize a "tough" policy toward Communism. His belief in the necessity of living continually in crisis, prepared for war, left its imprint on Soviet-American relations during the cold war period. Quite apart from the question of whether Forrestal's policies of suspicion and toughness will be praised or damned by future historians, we may ask whether those policies have any childhood roots. Emphasis has been placed on Forrestal's weak-father, dominant-mother family environment, which may have posed a childhood situation lacking in affection, in which it was difficult to establish a male identity. Did his quest for that male identity affect his political behavior and hence American foreign policy? "In Forrestal's world of foreign policy and military problems involving the Soviet bloc, to be militant was to be masculine." [38]

These are dramatic people performing dramatically—and they may have had dramatic childhoods. Although their stories provide some suggestion of the importance of childhood socialization for elite behavior, they do not really provide systematic evidence. Particularly, they refer only to the famous few at the very top. Do the principles of childhood socialization extend to the broader political elite?

Some attempt has been made to address this problem systematically. It is by now common knowledge that elites—even in democratic nations—are drawn disproportionately from higher social classes and from particular professions—notably the law. This "social bias" in the composition of political elites is profoundly disturbing to some, for it suggests inequality of opportunity, if not overt and deliberate discrimination against certain kinds of people. No doubt there is considerable truth in this, but differences in recruitment may be as well a result of political socialization; that is, of who gets socialized to *want* to be in the elite. When does interest in becoming, or willingness to become, a political figure arise? Childhood experiences may provide part of the answer. A recent study of the members of four American state legislatures demonstrated that 52 per cent of this elite group became interested in politics either as children or as adolescents. The inference that "state legislators tend to come from families which are much more involved in politics than the average American family,"[39] is buttressed by other work indicating that state legislators recall more childhood socialization experiences than lobbyists—persons who occupy a lesser political role.[40] In countries where political conflict is more heated than it is in the United States, the role of childhood socialization in the lives of legislative elites appears to be even more pronounced.[41] The more deeply citizens of a country hold political viewpoints, the more fervently older generations will try to indoctrinate the next.

Of course, even more obviously than is the case for mass behavior, childhood experiences cannot account for everything political elites do. Indeed, it is obvious that for many members of the legislative elite, interest develops during adulthood. Further, it is clear that childhood socialization cannot "anticipate" everything that is likely to happen to someone fully in the throes of active politics. Though childhood experiences may help determine that an individual will become a member of an elite, it is not likely to provide learning that will relate to the very specialized behavior required in specific elite positions. It is difficult to imagine what children would learn that would dispose them to be, say, an effective senator as opposed to an effective member of the House of Representatives.

If childhood socialization is not responsible, how does a person learn to become a judge, a bureaucrat, or a legislator? How does he learn the requirements of a specialized elite role? The obvious answer is adult socialization. But considering the very specialized kind of behavior involved, it must be very specialized socialization. In fact, it may be that the institution or people surrounding the role socialize new recruits as they arrive. Congress may socialize the newcomer, and the freshman judge may have a great deal to learn from his established colleagues. Party committees may have a great many directives for the neophyte. Socialization to specialized political elite roles turns out to be a fairly standard practice. It is a commonplace that all organizations, formal or informal, political or not, develop internal norms and standards to which members are urged to conform so that the organization can accomplish its objectives. If every member of a party, legislature, or administrative bureau indulged his own personal sentiments all of the time, chaos would reign and no collective goals would be realized.

Perhaps the most thoroughly researched example of this kind of institutional socialization involves the United States Congress. Two rules related to the idea of task accomplishment are apprenticeship and legislative work specialization. New members are expected to refrain from excessive floor debate and to perform dull and menial legislative tasks. A considerable period elapses in which newcomers quietly demonstrate that they are respectful of other (older) members and are fully trustworthy. Given the tremendous volume of legislation that Congress tries to consider each session, it is not hard to see why mutual respect and trust would be valued. Further, rather than attracting attention through public exposure, congressmen are expected to devote much attention and energy to committee assignments. Again, this rather unglamorous work must be done. Specialization is much valued in this regard also. A congressman who is an expert on economics and who works hard on the Banking and Currency Committee —for example, determining how businessmen would be likely to react to new restrictions on interest rates—would be much more encouraged than one who worked little, but made floor speeches on everything of interest.

Suppose congressmen don't find these arrangements to their liking? Sanctions can be imposed. Such members are not recognized; they are passed over for appointment to committees, and their efforts at introducing legislation or otherwise exerting influence are frustrated. Many new members find the directive "to get along, go along," quite compelling. But perhaps more important than overt sanctions are considerations that affect all political socialization. People have a need to accept standards; they have a need to relate to other people. Such standards are necessary to gain some sense of identity in the world. Families appear to be successful standard providers for children—indeed, we all admit that some agency must be. There is no reason in the world why legislative houses should not do so also.[42]

While not all elite political learning can be neatly categorized as childhood socialization or elite-role socialization, it is a convenient distinction to make. It emphasizes that in order to adequately account for the specialized behavior of people who are deeply involved politically, it is necessary to consider adult socialization quite seriously. Although one should definitely be aware of this—in fact, one should never lose sight of the fact that even mass behavior necessarily has some roots in adult socialization—our focus in this volume is largely on childhood. Accordingly, we will refer to elite socialization only when necessary to make a special point or to provide an example.

In describing the basic orientations to which people are socialized, this chapter has tried to indicate why political socialization is important and why its influence should be considered by every student of politics. It seems clear that political socialization has implications for every kind of politics. It is difficult to imagine any political event—from the very trivial to the most momentous—that may not have some connection to a political socialization experience. But knowing the kinds of political orientations people may hold is only a beginning. We need to look into the dynamics of the process of political socialization and also at its limits. Such an analysis—a more detailed examination of how socialization takes place—is the subject of the rest of this book.

NOTES

1. Fred I. Greenstein, "Political Socialization," in *International Encyclopedia of the Social Sciences,* vol. 14 (New York: Macmillan Co., 1968), pp. 552–53.
2. David Easton and Robert Hess, "The Child's Political World," *Midwest Journal of Political Science,* 6 (August 1962): 229–31.
3. See a discussion of this hypothesis in Dean Jaros, "Children's Orientations Toward the President: Some Additional Theoretical Considerations and Data," *Journal of Politics,* 30 (May 1967): 373–75.
4. David Easton and Jack Dennis, *Children in the Political System* (New York: McGraw-Hill Book Co., 1969), pp. 177–91; Fred I. Greenstein, "The Benevolent Leader: Children's Images of Political Authority," *American Political Science Review,* 54 (December 1960): 934–43.
5. David Easton, *A Systems Analysis of Political Life* (New York: John Wiley & Sons, 1965).
6. Easton and Dennis, *op. cit.,* pp. 58–59.
7. Richard E. Dawson and Kenneth Prewitt, *Political Socialization* (Boston: Little, Brown & Co., 1969), pp. 44–45.
8. Robert D. Hess and Judith V. Torney, *The Development of Political Attitudes in Children* (Chicago: Aldine Publishing Co., 1967), pp. 26–31; Gustav Jahoda, "The Development of Children's Ideas About Country and Nationality, Part II; National Symbols and Themes," *British Journal of Educational Psychology,* 33 (May 1963): 143–53.
9. Easton and Hess, *op. cit.;* Leonard Doob, *Patriotism and Nationalism* (New Haven: Yale University Press, 1964), pp. 24–36.
10. Edwin D. Lawson, "Development of Patriotism in Children: A Second Look," *Journal of Social Psychology,* 55 (April 1963): 279–86; Hess and Torney, *op. cit.*
11. Easton and Hess, *op. cit.,* p. 239.
12. Judith Gallatin and Joseph Adelson, "Individual Rights and the Public Good: A Cross-National Study of Adolescents," *Comparative Political Studies,* 3 (July 1970): 229.
13. Joseph Adelson and Robert O'Neill, "The Growth of Political Ideas in Adolescence: The Sense of Community," *Journal of Personality and Social Psychology,* 4 (July 1966): 295–306.
14. Edward S. Greenberg, "Black Children and the Political System: A Study of Socialization to Support," *Public Opinion Quarterly,* 34 (Fall 1970): 333–46.
15. Fred I. Greenstein and Sidney G. Tarrow, "The Study of French Political Socialization: Toward the Revocation of Paradox," *World Politics,* 22 (October 1969): 107–10.
16. Easton and Dennis, *op. cit.,* p. 240.
17. Edward S. Greenberg, "Children and Government: A Comparison Across Racial Lines," *Midwest Journal of Political Science,* 14 (May 1970): 249–70.
18. Harrell R. Rodgers and George Taylor, "The Policeman as an Agent of Regime Legitimation," *Midwest Journal of Political Science,* 15 (February 1971): 72–86.
19. Edward S. Greenberg, "Orientations of Black and White Children to Political Authority Figures," *Social Science Quarterly,* 51 (December 1970): 561–71.
20. Rodgers and Taylor, *op. cit.*
21. David Easton and Jack Dennis, "The Child's Acquisition of Regime Norms: Political Efficacy," *American Political Science Review,* 61 (March 1967): 30.

22. Gallatin and Adelson, *op. cit.*

23. Schley R. Lyons, "The Political Socialization of Ghetto Children: Efficacy and Cynicism," *Journal of Politics,* 32 (May 1970): 288–304.

24. Fred I. Greenstein, *Children and Politics* (New Haven: Yale University Press, 1965), p. 127.

25. Jack Dennis et al., "Political Socialization to Democratic Orientations in Four Western Systems," *Comparative Political Studies,* 1 (April 1968): 81.

26. *Ibid.,* p. 87.

27. Angus Campbell et. al., *The American Voter* (New York: John Wiley & Sons, 1960), pp. 216–65.

28. Greenstein, *Children and Politics,* p. 66; Robert D. Hess and David Easton, "The Child's Changing Image of the President," *Public Opinion Quarterly,* 24 (Winter 1960): 637–38.

29. Hess and Torney, *op. cit.,* chap. 4.

30. Easton and Dennis, *Children in the Political System,* p. 203.

31. Greenstein, *Children and Politics,* p. 69.

32. M. Kent Jennings and Richard Niemi, "Family Structure and the Transmission of Political Values," *American Political Science Review,* 62 (March 1968): 169–84.

33. Greenstein, *Children and Politics,* p. 70.

34. Hess and Torney, *op. cit.,* p. 90; Greenstein, *Children and Politics,* p. 73.

35. Jack Dennis and Donald J. McCrone, "Preadult Development of Political Party Identification in Western Democracies," *Comparative Political Studies,* 3 (July 1970): 243–62.

36. Alexander L. George and Juliette L. George, *Woodrow Wilson and Colonel House: A Personality Study* (New York: John Day, 1956).

37. David Shub, *Lenin* (Garden City, New York: Doubleday & Co., 1948), pp. 13–16.

38. Arnold A. Rogow, "James Forrestal: An Appraisal," in *Psychology and Politics,* Leroy N. Rieselbach and George I. Balch, eds. (New York: Holt, Rinehart & Winston, 1969), p. 285.

39. John Wahlke et al., *The Legislative System* (New York: John Wiley & Sons, 1962), p. 82.

40. Harmon Zeigler and Michael A. Baer, *Lobbying* (Belmont, Calif.: Wadsworth Publishing Co., 1969), p. 49.

41. Allan Kornberg and Norman Thomas, "The Political Socialization of National Legislative Elites in the United States and Canada," *Journal of Politics,* 27 (November 1965): 768.

42. Malcolm Jewell and Samuel C. Patterson, *The Legislative Process in the United States* (New York: Random House, 1966), chap. 15.

3. Limits of Childhood Socialization: Continuous Learning

Although we can convincingly argue that childhood mass socialization has a definite impact on adult political behavior, we should be prepared to think about the *limits* of childhood socialization as a determinant of political behavior. Learning may not be restricted to children. If, as we have just seen, socialization to the specialized political roles elites perform may occur during adulthood, is it not possible that some kinds of *mass* socialization may also occur during adulthood? That is, socialization may be a continuous process extending throughout the life cycle. This raises the possibility that early socialization may be displaced or overriden by later socialization, nullified by adult experiences or even by deliberate countersocialization. It also raises the possibility—probably more important—that childhood socialization on any dimension may be "incomplete." That is, what an individual learns as a child may not provide him with guidelines for behavior in every political situation he encounters as an adult. A child may acquire party identification as well as the capacity to understand political issues. But how is he prepared for an adult situation in which he must (by referendum) opt for or against a proposal for city-county merger? No guiding principles may have been implanted during childhood. Similarly, the complexities of adult life may result in conflict situations for which early acquired political principles are totally inadequate. A classic example might be the case where a British youth is brought up to believe in the Conservative Party but also that proud Britain should never become economically tied to the European continent. What is he to do when, upon reaching adulthood, he discovers his party actively promoting entry to the Common Market? Childhood socialization provides no answer.

There are two basic considerations that could result in the erosion or "failure" of childhood political socialization. These are "generational" change and "maturational" change. Generational change simply refers to the fact that changes in attitude, values, and behavior are likely to occur from one generation to another. Each generation experiences events not felt by those either younger or older. It may be expected to bear a characteristic imprint of those events—an imprint not shared by previous or subsequent generations. The generation now in its fifties experienced the dramatic, disrupting, and fully emotion- and energy-consuming event of World War II in a way that could only result in great mental changes, which of necessity created a "generation gap" between their older counterparts and themselves. The current generation gap, though often overemphasized, is a similar phenomenon. People in their twenties have grown up in and lived in circumstances—affluence, technological advancement, mass communication—experienced by no previous generation. It is not difficult to understand that they would be, in part, different kinds of people.

Maturational change simply means that as people grow older, they find themselves in new conditions or possessing new attributes. Formal education changes in character and ultimately ends. The end of adolescence is typically accompanied by great increases in responsibility, especially to family and children. Physical strength and stamina increase to a peak and then decline. Ultimately, ability to work and earn a livelihood is impaired. It is impossible to think that people's values, beliefs, and norms are totally unaffected by the different circumstances which maturation brings. Many of them, it is clear, are of tremendous significance.

GENERATIONAL CHANGE AND POLITICAL SOCIALIZATION

In some societies and at some periods of history, very little generational change takes place. Many primitive societies whose ways have scarcely changed in recent centuries still exist, untouched by industrialization and modernization. Since the potential life circumstances of the young are little different from their parents', there is scant impetus toward rejection of the values and orientations to which the older generation socializes them. In some historical periods—for example, the Middle Ages—the whole world was characterized by few, if any, generational differences.

Of course, most of today's world is in just the opposite situation. Indeed, we are now experiencing the most rapid change—and the rate of change is increasing all the time—that the world has ever known. Propelled by a dramatically advancing technology, change is everywhere. Social change is not excepted from this great contemporary dynamic. It would be amazing indeed if what one generation taught its offspring about politics were always congruent with future realities. What could would-be socializers of the 1940's, for example, have taught their young about reacting to television which was to be the most significant and widespread form of political communication the younger generation would experience? The answer, of course, is nothing, for television was virtually unknown to that older generation.

Mobility. As we become more affluent, more industrialized, and possessed of more efficient transportation, we are becoming a much more mobile society, not only geographically, but socially, too. Geographical mobility implies that people are much less likely to live out their entire lives in their "hometown" than they were even a few years ago. The demand of corporate transfer practices, the lure of improved conditions, have set off a virtual stampede of people and a parade of moving vans. People now change jobs or locations with great frequency. Is what a person learned at his parents' knee about the politics of Green Bay, Wisconsin, going to serve him to interact in the politics of Spartanburg, South Carolina? To be sure, both Green Bay and Spartanburg are part of a general American political milieu. As such, they share some commonalities of institutional structure; and surely the citizens of both communities hold in common some attitudes toward the appropriate nature and scope of the functions of government. On the other hand, there are important regional differences in political experiences, traditions, expectations, and norms within the United States. As these cities are located within different regional contexts, it is reasonable to expect considerable divergence in political practice and in values concerning government. To the extent that these divergences represent incompatibilities or inconsistencies, a person moving from one community to the other may experience difficulty. New political learning—that is, adult political socialization—may be an absolute necessity.

The present great interregional migration—similar ones have been frequent in American history—began in this country about thirty-five years ago. Massive movements of blacks and less affluent whites from the South to the North and West and of more affluent whites from the North to the South and West continue to the present day. Although it is clear that migrants do bring some of their earlier socialized politics with them when they move (e.g., party identification),[1] it is only a partial process. For example, a young business executive transferring to the South may find that his new suburban environment is quite different from his old suburban environment. Instead of a city manager, he finds no municipal executive because there is no municipality at all where he lives. Instead of a board of county commissioners, he finds a "fiscal court" exercising legislative functions. Additional socialization is very likely to occur.

The entire modern period of history has been characterized by migration from rural to urban areas. This is true of the contemporary United States as well as most of the rest of the world. It is conventional wisdom that rural migrants to urban areas are unprepared for their new environments. They experience great contrast and their lives are disrupted. It is equally conventional wisdom that such rural newcomers must learn fast (i.e., undergo socialization) if they are to survive. Since their new politics—involving remote city officials whom they cannot personally know, perhaps intergovernmental relations, and policies designed to deal with problems never even thought of before—is also unfamiliar, they must learn in this area, too.

Perhaps one of the most dramatic political phenomena in recent American history is related to urban migration. This is the great increase in black protest activity that has taken place in the last fifteen years or so. Why should organization, political activity, and even violence occur now rather than in the 1920's, when, if anything, the conditions under which blacks lived were generally worse? Part of the answer must be that the contemporary black is exposed to adult socialization influences that were largely absent a generation ago. These new influences result from urbanism. The demand for a larger urban work force with its promise of better employment, plus displacement from agricultural jobs by new kinds of farm equipment, stimulated a great influx of blacks from the rural South to the urban North. Instead of being thinly spread all over the South, blacks now are concentrated in cities. The fact of concentration alone (increased by effective confinement to ghetto areas) has socialization implications. Contact with other blacks, including those already educated and sophisticated by urban life, was now possible. Organization and collective action could now reasonably be discussed; previous socialization agents could not even have conceived of the possibility. Living in urban areas and exposed to mass media, blacks could learn more about the dominant white culture and a great deal more about the extent to which they really are deprived. The political importance of this kind of cognitive socialization cannot be underestimated. Only when this new socialization occurred could people, socialized to a posture of rural passivity as children, undertake a new and dynamic kind of political behavior.[2]

Social mobility refers to changing social class or status rather than physical movement (though, of course, people sometimes relocate in an attempt to improve class or status). With a rapidly expanding economy and great increases in the total wealth available, change is inevitable. Moreover, as society and technology become more complex, people who possess mechanical, technical, or managerial skills become more valuable; only if these skills are applied can any progress be made. Accordingly, rewards are given more and more on the basis of skill and accomplishment than on the basis of family heritage or social rank. New wealth is parceled out on a different basis than previously, and status shifts necessarily follow. The great spread of education also contributes to this process. More people have access to the skills that lead to success. We are all familiar with the young person from a family of very modest means who is able to get a college education and thus achieve higher status employment and greater wealth than his parents. This has become a frequent occurrence, an example of prevalent *upward* status mobility. Downward mobility is also possible. For example, imagine a young man born into a wealthy family, the son of the owner, say, of a small metals plating firm. Shortly after taking over the family business, however, he finds that new antipollution regulations are increasing his costs. Being relatively incompetent, he is unable to cope with the changed circumstances, and his firm fails. His income and status decline greatly. Given his relative incompetence, he cannot do particularly well as the employee of another firm, so his downward mobility is confirmed. However, far more widespread is *relative* downward status mobility. This is the case where one person or group remains relatively constant in income or status or gains only slowly while many others advance rapidly. White industrial workers in the United States are clearly not in a condition of absolute decline; indeed, they are becoming more affluent each year. However, these workers may perceive that blacks, Puerto Ricans, and chicanos, while objectively of lower status than themselves, are progressing at an accelerated rate. These previously lower-status groups are closing the gap. Hence, the white worker experiences relative downward mobility.

Downward mobility, absolute or relative, may indeed have dramatic political behavioral effects. There is some evidence that such changes are so traumatic that their victims, suffering from what some researchers call "status anxiety," seek out right-wing groups. Unable to cope with new circumstances, these people are willing to accept new political norms, a new explanation for their unfortunate situation, and a set of new programs to rectify the situation. They are ready, it might be argued, to accept adult political socialization. Right-wing groups are, of course, anxious to act as socialization agents and are apparently somewhat successful. Thus, socialization to right-wing political views may have nothing whatever to do with norms acquired in childhood. Instead, it may be a function of adult-level socialization for which people were prepared by downward mobility.[3]

Similarly, the more numerous upwardly mobile may find themselves in situations for which their childhood political socialization in no way prepared them. Of course, it is a commonplace that upwardly mobile people suddenly find that they have objective *interests* at variance with their past and so reject early teachings. The businessman from humble beginnings decides that the welfare state is now repugnant to him and his profit potential, despite the fact that he grew up believing in it and even benefiting from some of its policies. Upwardly mobile people—who are very anxious about moving up—also seem to engage in *anticipatory socialization.* That is, they try to find out what behavior is typical of persons in the higher status position and then, rejecting their previous norms, try to imitate that behavior. As if to insure themselves a place in the desired status grouping, people supposedly allow themselves to be socialized by this grouping even though they have not yet "made it."

The upward mobility of current generations can in these ways dramatically limit the efficacy of childhood political socialization. But there are other dynamics as well—dynamics that do not necessarily imply rejection of lower-class norms, but indicate instead that lower-class socialization is often not extensive enough to cover contingencies encountered by the middle class. Middle-class people are directly affected by a variety of complex government policies—regulation of securities trade, awarding of government contracts, support for higher education, adjustments in levels of property taxation, and so forth—that are more relevant to middle-class life than to working-class life. There is thus an impetus toward greater involvement in politics, an impetus reinforced by the middle-class man's superior education, which enables him to understand the impact of politics on his life. Of course, lower-class childhood socialization does not prepare a person for this expanded scope of political interest, so the mobile man must learn as he goes. Similarly, middle-class people are asked to participate politically to a much larger extent. They serve on commissions, advisory boards, and juries, while working-class persons by and large do not. Working-class childhood socialization teaches nothing of such roles; the mobile person cannot rely on his past for guidance.[4]

Political and Historical Events. As we suggested earlier in this chapter, dramatic historical events leave a deep imprint on the generations during whose lives they happen. This is so because earlier socialization cannot provide any preparation for the great changes that such crises cause; would-be socializers are necessarily very parochial agents who cannot foresee the political future. No childhood socialization could have prepared anyone for the economic cataclysm of the great Depression of the 1930's. Existing norms about how to evaluate candidates and public policy seemed pointless and inappropriate in this crisis. Accordingly, much new socialization occurred. Much of it emanated from the then-current administration, which had at its disposal socialization instruments—for example, the mass medium of radio—likely to be effective in times of crisis. Indeed, there is a "Depression generation" that was particularly susceptible to the adult socialization influences surrounding this event. Party identification, for example, underwent widespread and drastic revision during this period. The age group that just reached adulthood at the time of the Depression is today more Democratic in its party identification than either previous or subsequent generations. This generation, now in its sixties, still stands out in surveys of voting.[5]

Incidentally, this generational effect was once frequently mistaken for a maturational effect. Voting studies conducted in the 1930's and 1940's discovered that the younger voters (i.e., the Depression generation) were more Democratic than older voters. This led, fairly logically, to the assumption that party preference was a function of age, which seems to conform to the old adage that as one gets older (matures), he becomes more conservative, for older people were Republicans (conservative) while younger ones were Democrats (liberal). Of course, this was a naive and erroneous conclusion. As the years passed and the Depression generation was no longer the youngest group of voters, the results of newer voting studies began to contradict earlier findings. It became clear that being young did not in itself contribute to being Democratic, nor being older to being Republican. The error was corrected as scholars realized they were looking at a generational phenomenon, not a maturational one.

An event that often produces tremendous change is war—especially for the losing side. The relevance of prewar socialization for postwar realities must often be problematical. Consider the plight of Arab peoples living in the Sinai peninsula. As youngsters, they may have been socialized toward many of the objects and practices of the United Arab Republic. They may have acquired a positive image of President Nasser and a love for symbols of the political community. As young adults they find, after a brief war, that they live under the political administration of Israel. Regardless of what posture the Arab ultimately takes toward his new political environment—one of resignation to the new rule or one of actively subversive hostility toward a regime regarded as temporary—he will have much political socialization to undergo as an adult. Almost any war must have this kind of impact on the generations who most immediately experience the change. Czechs, in the years prior to 1914, must have been politically socialized largely in terms of the Austro-Hugarian empire. After World War I, however, they discovered that the victorious powers had imposed a new political community on them—Czechoslovakia. What did this new entity mean? How was it to be run? How should citizens relate to it? Empire-oriented childhood socialization could provide no answers. Adult socialization was necessary. Or consider the generation-to-generation continuity of political socialization in pre-World War II Japan, where children had been taught for centuries that the emperor was a sacred political figure.[6] Imagine how different the situation was for the generations that experienced crushing military defeat, virtual annihilation of the regime, American military occupation, and the institution of a totally different kind of politics. The dramatic differences between prewar and postwar Japan bear testimony to the fact that much, much political learning had to be experienced by adults.

Revolution would have much the same sort of consequences. Childhood socialization occurring in the old regime is simply irrelevant to the new. In fact, many revolutionary regimes clearly recognize this fact and consciously try to provide political education programs for adults to eliminate the discontinuity and promote norms which support the new regime.[7]

Some Immediate Problems. Mobility and political events impose perhaps their most dramatic limitations on childhood political socialization in the new nations of the world that have recently achieved national independence. Most of these nations are attempting to develop modern economies, which necessitates urbanization, new kinds of employment, and different ways of life along almost every dimension. The degree of mobility required —from remote back-country villages to newly built cities, from primitive hunter or tiller to foundry laborer or government agency clerk—must be great indeed. The number of new rules and practices staggers the imagination of one who has lived all his life in a relatively unchanging culture. These nations illustrate vividly the problems of new communities—indeed, the achievement of national independence is one of the crucial community-level political concerns of recent decades—for most of these areas have traditionally had a much less elaborate form of politics, one focused on local, tribal loyalties and identification. The inadequacy of early socialization to deal with problems of basic community identification is a continuous challenge for new nations.[8]

Although it is easy to see how generational change can be dramatic and disruptive in the rapidly developing areas of the world, we ought to consider that even the industrialized West may be in for a period of great generational change. Because of new technology, experiences that future generations have may be radically different than their predecessors' were. The imprint of these experiences may then create a "supergeneration gap"—a gap that increases with each successive generation. There are those who believe that we are on the verge of such momentous change that virtually all present norms, beliefs, and forms of social behavior will be irrelevant. Childhood socialization under the impact of such "future shock" would be totally inefficacious. For example, it is often noted (sometimes with dark pessimism, sometimes with new hope, depending on individual preferences) that human feelings, emotions, beliefs, and behavior may come to be heavily determined by drugs. There is no question that new psychoactive (mind-altering) drugs have had a dramatic impact on psychotherapy. In general, stays in mental hospitals are much shorter than they once were because drugs enable patients who formerly were required to be confined to hospitals to display more "socially acceptable" behavior. In short, therapists can get people to do what they want by giving them drugs. The great use of "tranquilizers" is a slightly less dramatic, but much more widespread, example of the same thing.[9] Various drug culture groups make elaborate claims for the ability of various substances to alter their users' politically relevant behavior. For example, LSD is supposed to make one a pacifist. Though these claims are in the main extreme and unfounded, other evidence suggests that pharmacological manipulations of political orientations is distinctly possible.[10] The 1971 president of the American Psychological Association has (apparently seriously) raised the possibility of administering drugs to world leaders to inhibit aggressive orientations toward international relations. Thus, new generations' political behavior may be dependent upon chemistry, not childhood socialization at all.

A similar possibility is raised by new research in genetics. It may be that knowledge of the human genetic processes may be on the verge of permitting the alteration of personality by interference with hereditary mechanisms. Of course, this raises the specter of fantastic political manipulation. As in Huxley's *Brave New World,* a race of conforming, passive, serving subjects could be constructed to do the bidding of scheming manipulators. But even if one does not carry the principle that far, the idea of producing, through "artificial" means, people who conform to some predetermined paradigm is abroad in the land and a matter for serious consideration. Happiness, quiescence, "adjustment," even specific desires and preferences, seem to be nearly within reach of conscious determination.[11]

Regardless of whether these bizarre and dramatic techniques of behavior determination become widespread realities, contemporary generations may face monumental forces, unknown to their predecessors, capable of imposing severe limits on childhood socialization. Many scholars believe that man cannot physically survive as a species under today's technology and social organization without radical change in human behavior patterns. We possess the power to destroy the world through environmental pollution. If we are not to do so, goes the argument, present orientations toward wealth, work, and economic organization cannot persist. Only radical transformation will suffice. Man must adapt in order to survive. Many believe that he *will* adapt. That, of course, requires new practices of many kinds, including political ones. It requires as well the rejection of old politics and with it the imperatives, for this generation, of childhood political socialization. A similar argument has often been made about international relations. Everyone has heard the suggestion that "nationalism is obsolete." The meaning of this notion is clear. In today's world, with widespread distribution of nuclear weapons, with destructive capabilities so great, with international economic and social intercourse growing by leaps and bounds, proponents of this argument would say that a posture of nationalism can only lead to destruction. Survival demands its abandonment.

Indeed, a logical concomitant of this line of reasoning is that socialization to *substantive* political orientations is obsolete. In the future, there must be socialization to acceptance of change, to the norms of adaptation and tolerance, if we are to survive. To the extent that the latter socialization is likely to occur in adulthood and the former in childhood, adaptive man must again reject political norms which perhaps he learned in childhood. If man will, in fact, be adaptive, and if the crisis of survival is as immediate and pressing as some thinkers suggest, then the displacement of childhood political socialization for the present generation seems a very real eventuality indeed.

MATURATIONAL CHANGE AND POLITICAL SOCIALIZATION

Just as times change and dramatic political events occur, so do people change and dramatic personal events occur in their lives as they grow older. Just as childhood socialization may be incomplete or inappropriate to new political conditions, so may childhood socialization be incomplete or inappropriate to the new conditions a person finds himself in as a consequence of aging. To be sure, the extent to which maturational change occurs is itself dependent in part on the nature of the times. The simpler and more primitive the culture, probably the less dramatic are the changes of age. In extended family systems, for example, young people never leave their parents and set up fully independent households. Of course, a more definite break in family relations is more typical of modern, industrialized cultures. But regardless of the society, some age-related change occurs. As individuals age, they occupy different roles; different expectations surround them, and they do different things. This is most obvious, perhaps, in sexual and employment behavior. Many maturational changes are universally thought to be very significant; some of them like puberty and marriage are the subject of celebration and rite. It is not unreasonable to think that the incongruities of maturation would have implications for the continued impact of political socialization. Let us examine some of the possibilities.

Intellectual Sophistication. As we noted in chapter 2, what people learn about the political world may partly depend on what they are capable of understanding. That simple childhood conceptions do not persist into adulthood is something we have noted frequently. Additions to the child's political world occur with age (e.g., issue orientation), and modifications of existing elements (e.g., images of the President) do also.

For our present purposes, it is significant to note that several interesting additions to, and modifications of, individuals' political orientations occur in early adulthood. Some of these may be due to increasing intellectual sophistication stemming not so much from growing cognitive capability as from increased learning. It should come as no surprise that recent research comparing high school seniors and adults showed the latter to possess considerably more knowledge about political affairs. One could perhaps interpret this greater learning as a function of a longer life span. Along with more information, adults are less trusting and more cynical about political office holders. It looks as if youthful idealism is still being ground off against abrasive reality in early adulthood. This type of change is similar to that observed in early to middle childhood.

A similar finding concerns party identification. We noted previously that very young children readily adopt a party preference without much in the way of supporting information. It is interesting, however, that the proportion of youngsters claiming to be *independents* generally increases throughout the school years, reaching a peak during twelfth grade. The decline in partisanship may well be a consequence of stressing the norm of independence in the schools. A desire to "stay out of politics" has traditionally characterized school officials in America. In any event, the growth of independence appears to stop with the end of high school, for adults are notably more partisan than seniors. They apparently reassert an original childhood preference. Again, perhaps we are witnessing the decline of an idealistic, proud, and free conscience. Socialization to political reality may be occurring in adulthood.

Greater political interest and greater attention to politics in newspapers and on television also characterize adults as opposed to high-schoolers. In summary, it would seem that adults, whose capacities are more highly developed, are capable of undergoing considerable political socialization at the government level. They respond to stimuli to which their younger counterparts do not.[12] To argue that the process of political socialization, at least in these realms, is substantially completed during childhood or even adolescence is clearly misleading. Early socialization is subject to modification.

Of course, not all of this maturational change is due to expanding intellectual capacities. Less sophistication may characterize younger people because it is a cultural norm to shield them from harsh reality. It is probably also true that adults try to shield children from all manifestations of human conflict. Divorce, lawsuits, crime, and war are probably among the phenomena that tend to be whitewashed. Politics in general may well be, too. We have already seen how the early images children hold are largely devoid of conflict. This is a curious picture of politics, but it may be that adults encourage youngsters to think in terms of milk-and-honey harmony, benevolent leaders, great consensus, and the benefit of all, rather than of winners and losers, the exercise of influence, manipulation of men in order to gain power, to say nothing of governmental inefficiency, corruption, and overt dishonesty.

That these early orientations must change is now obvious. But an extremely interesting question is, What are the consequences of what must be a tremendous disillusionment? Can the shock cause a dramatic reaction? Many believe that it can and does. The relatively low level of adult political participation in the United States may result, in part, from the fact that voting is usually the only political participatory act that is stressed during childhood. The great emphasis on voting, particularly in the schools, has already been discussed. It is easy to see that, when this emphasis is coupled with a strong norm of independence, youngsters might come to believe that political decisions conform on a one-to-one basis with rationally expressed preferences of a majority of citizens. When it becomes obvious to the adolescent or young adult that this is but a caricature of politics, he may lapse into apathy. Of course, the schools are sometimes faulted for presenting a naive majoritarianism and for creating a false belief in the efficacy of voting. Even though organizational activity and party work, for example, are likely to have a more direct bearing on policy outcomes, we suggest to our young that pressure groups are somehow perversions of the democratic process and insist that they should "vote for the man" and eschew party labels. When maturation reveals that simple voting does not dictate all actions of politicians, but that interest groups and party regulars do have much impact, disillusionment and withdrawal may be a likely result.

A similar explanation has been advanced to account for contemporary youth protest. The political world does not correspond to what young people have been taught it should be. Disillusionment in this case leads to quite dramatic activity rather than withdrawal. Such protest is occurring now rather than in the past because political life is changing at a faster rate than during any other period in history; life in industrial society of the 1970's has become fantastically complex. (Here, this explanation employs elements of a generational approach as well as a maturational one.) The involvement of multiple levels of government in given problems is now commonplace. Responsibility for welfare policy, which was once a local matter, is today distributed among a great number of agencies—federal, state, and local. Public-private arrangements are now common, like those for passenger rail service. New policies are assumed by government in such areas as pollution control and automotive safety. In short, as each year passes, our modern society becomes more and more complicated and intricate. It is increasingly difficult to understand political arrangements. Politics deviates more and more from the naive, juvenile image we held as children. Political maturation may now be such a momentous experience that protest behavior is an understandable consequence.

Adolescent Rebellion. A slightly different maturational theme is expressed in the idea of adolescent rebellion. In most modern societies, children must move from a position of complete dependence on their parents to one of eventual complete autonomy. This calls for a drastic adjustment on the part of both parents and children in their relationship to one another. These adjustments, particularly father-son adjustments, occur typically in later adolescence. Children believe themselves old enough to behave as adults. It is necessary for them to assert independence, to show that relations with parents have changed. This can entail direct challenging of the parents and overt rejection of the values they hold.

This thesis has been used to interpret radical political movements such as Communism and German fascism. Even contemporary youth protest in America has been described as a direct consequence of rage against the father. Many of these explanations are clearly inadequate, and it appears that the adolescent-rebellion notion has often been used not for its ability to add to our understanding but to invoke feelings of high drama. Nonetheless, it is true that most movements for political change disproportionately involve the young. Perhaps the rebellion hypothesis does contain a grain of truth; in any event, it would be foolish to reject it out of hand.

Most systematic, serious observers, however, find little indication—at least as far as the United States is concerned—that childhood political socialization is likely to be swept away by a wave of adolescent rebellion. Young people's government-level attitudes do not appear to represent a rejective posture toward their parents (indeed, there is a high degree of similarity), in-depth interviews fail to reveal momentous political clashes with parents, and radical students today appear to be acting *congruently* with their parents' (unfulfilled) principles rather than in opposition to them.[13] Most research seems to indicate that if this notion has any validity at all, there are many circumstances under which it can be rendered inoperative. In a permissive society, such as that in the United States, there may be less "need" to rebel. There is no need for a "war of independence" under such conditions. Even if rebellion takes place, it is quite likely that it will be channeled into areas other than politics. In the United States, interest and participation in politics are low. Accordingly, an adolescent is unlikely to assert his independence over political values that are relatively unimportant to his parents. Something else, like the educational or career aspirations the parents hold for the adolescent, may be the target of rebellion.[14]

Thus, it appears that adolescent rebellion is not a form of maturational change that has a widespread political impact in this country. However, assuming that the general principle is valid, it is quite possible that in cultures which are less permissive with their children or in those where politics is more salient, politically directed rebellion could constitute quite a severe limit on childhood socialization. But until we know more about whether rebellion really occurs and more about such cultures, we must suspend judgment.

Changing Roles. "He who is not a Communist at twenty has no heart; he who is still a Communist at forty has no head." This statement about maturational change in politics is sometimes made about domestic politics in Western Europe. Regardless of whether one thinks it contains any profound wisdom, the implication is clear. Young people, not yet jaded by harsh experience, can be idealistic and allow themselves to be governed by their emotions. Aging, however, results in disillusionment; responsibilities must be assumed, work must be done; that which is possible must be accomplished, ideals must be forgotten. Although many will find this an unduly cynical statement, which argues against any change, it does suggest a kind of maturational development that appears to occur quite frequently. There is no doubt that people are thrust into different situations as they mature and that these different situations are surrounded by varying expectations. Again, it seems quite unlikely that new expectations surrounding new roles would be entirely without effect on the behavior of individuals.

It is commonly assumed that one of the great age-related changes of political attitudes is increasing conservatism. Due to increasing responsibility, increasing wealth, declining idealism, or increasing general rigidity, older people are thought to vote for conservative parties and to generally resist change. We have already seen that this assertion is at least partially false. There is no evidence that Democrats abandon their party for the Republican as they age, nor can one support the notion that liberal political principles are abandoned with maturity. Data showing that younger people hold more liberal or leftist views can probably be attributed to generational change, not to maturational change. Thus, there is no particular likelihood that a child socialized to liberal ideology will outgrow his political ideals. New roles only rarely shake substantive political beliefs.

There is, however, a certain "nonsubstantive" conservatism that does appear to increase with age. Older people are less likely to deviate from the political principles to which they have been socialized, regardless of whether these principles are liberal or conservative. That is to say, an older liberal is likely to be a more inflexible liberal; an older conservative is likely to be a more inflexible conservative. It is easy to understand this growing investment in one's personal status quo. The longer a person stands for something, the more associates who are supportive of his beliefs he will have. Men become increasingly associated with a position, and expectations that they will uphold that position grow.[15]

An important consequence of this kind of maturational conservatism is that youth must be the predominant carrier of political change. New issues, new personalities are more likely to generate responses in younger people. The young are more volatile (and less predictable) and more impressionable, because they are constrained by fewer expectations. Everything from "trends" for or against a given candidate in an election to dramatic political and historical events operate mainly through changes in the behavior of youth.

Probably the most significant maturational role changes have to do with increasing political involvement. It is well known that, at least in periods of relative calm, older people are more participatory in politics. In fact—contrary to popular belief—the youngest citizens are in general the least participatory. Maturing citizens are progressively more participatory until their sixties, when physical infirmities begin to restrict level of participation. Involvement rests on initiation to adult roles as well as on childhood socialization. The adult is employed; he is directly taxed. This is likely to result in some concern with government expenditures and policy. The adult owns a home and other property. Local government (a topic of very little interest to the young, who favor the drama of national and international affairs) suddenly becomes highly salient, as do public education and its politics. Greater involvement in the form of voting or petitioning is likely to result.

Although it is true that many people encounter dramatically new life circumstances as they get older, there are many conditions under which basic goal orientations remain the same over long periods, perhaps even complete life spans. But even within an unchanging basic goal orientation, people may encounter changing roles and thus undergo differential socialization. For example, we know that children come early to value political participation (rule by the people). Later, they become aware of some behavior on this dimension (voting). But it is quite likely that awareness of, for example, organizational activity and ability to carry it out arrive quite late. Many adults are astonished to think that forming a "civic organization" is an effective way to prevent the state from diverting a stream, say, or from raising water bills. Moreover, many do not have the slightest notion of how to go about it—unless some more knowledgeable person socializes them.

Although it is likely that what adults do in politics is related to how they were socialized as children, it is clearly wrong to anticipate that a person's political self is fully determined by the end of childhood and unchanging thereafter. Childhood political learning, we have seen, may be overridden; new political learning may replace the old. Childhood socialization may be incomplete in that it does not anticipate all the contingencies of adult political life. Both generational change and maturational change are certain in the modern world, and these are bound to impose limits on the efficacy of childhood determinants of political behavior.

But by no means should we regard these limits as undermining the whole study of childhood political socialization. On the contrary, since these limits imply the existence of later socialization, they may prove to be of great value to the student of childhood learning. By studying limits, we are studying processes of socialization. If we know something about how later counter-socialization proceeds, we may be able to extrapolate backward in time and gain some insights as to how early primary socialization comes about. In any event, the question of how people become socialized—that is, who are the agents of socialization and what are the processes by which they influence the young— is clearly one of critical importance. If we are to understand and explain political socialization in any complete sense, we must address these questions directly. It is to that task that we now turn.

NOTES

1. Philip E. Converse, "On the Possibility of Major Political Realignment in the South," in *Change in the Contemporary South,* Allan P. Sindler, ed. (Durham, N.C.: Duke University Press, 1963), pp. 195–222.
2. Jack R. Van Der Slik, ed., *Black Conflict with White America* (Columbus, Ohio: Charles E. Merrill Publishing Co., 1970), pt. I.
3. Fred W. Grupp, Jr., "The Political Perspectives of Birch Society Members," in *The American Right Wing,* Robert A. Schoenberger, ed. (New York: Holt, Rinehart & Winston, 1969), p. 98.
4. See, on this point, David O. Sears, "Political Behavior," in *The Handbook of Social Psychology,* Gardner Lindzey and Elliot Aronson, eds., vol. 5, 2d ed. (Reading, Mass.: Addison-Wesley Publishing Co., 1969), pp. 383–85; Orville Brim and Stanton Wheeler, *Socialization After Childhood* (New York: John Wiley & Sons, 1966), pp. 83–98; Robert E. Lane, *Political Life* (Glencoe, Ill.: Free Press, 1959), pp. 220–34.
5. Angus Campbell et al., *The American Voter* (New York: John Wiley & Sons, 1960), pp. 153–56.
6. Akira Kubota and Robert E. Ward, "Family Influence and Political Socialization in Japan: Some Preliminary Findings in Comparative Perspective," *Comparative Political Studies,* 3 (July 1970): 140–75.
7. Richard E. Dawson and Kenneth Prewitt, *Political Socialization* (Boston: Little, Brown & Co., 1969), p. 95.
8. *Ibid.,* pp. 96–97.
9. Albert Somit, "Towards a More Biologically Oriented Political Science: Ethnology and Psychopharmacology," *Midwest Journal of Political Science,* 12 (August 1968): 550.

10. Dean Jaros, "Biochemical Desocialization: Depressants and Political Behavior," *Midwest Journal of Political Science,* 16 (February 1972): 1–22.

11. On many of these points see the semipopular work by Alvin Toffler, *Future Shock* (New York: Random House, 1970). On the specific point of genetic manipulation see pp. 197–209.

12. M. Kent Jennings and Richard Niemi, "Patterns of Political Learning," *Harvard Educational Review,* 38 (Summer 1968): 443–67.

13. Jeanne Block, Norma Haan, and M. Brewster Smith, "Activism and Apathy in Contemporary Adolescents," in *Understanding Adolescence,* James F. Adams, ed. (Boston: Allyn & Bacon, 1968), pp. 214–15.

14. Robert E. Lane, "Fathers and Sons: Foundations of Political Belief," *American Sociological Review,* 24 (August 1959): 502–11.

15. Sears, *op. cit.,* p. 399.

4. The Socializers:
The Parental Family

We live in dynamic times. Change is everywhere. Political systems arise and die, revolutions overturn established regimes, wars disrupt the lives of millions. But juxtaposed with this universal condition of flux are some astonishing examples of political persistence. Many nations, for example Great Britain and Japan, have existed continuously for centuries. Republican-Democrat dominance of the American two-party system has been a fact of political life for well over a century. Many other examples of political continuity come easily to mind. It is clear that some kinds of intergenerational transmission of political norms has been occurring on a regular basis. Some "conservatizing" agents of political socialization are clearly effectively at work.

As noted in chapter 1, one of the most prominent of such socializers is the family. Many established leaders have regarded the family as an important device for communicating the political values of the dominant culture, while all revolutionary figures have feared the family as a brake on social change. Indeed, modern revolutionary regimes have taken quite dramatic steps to limit the impact of the family on children. Soviet child care arrangements, for example, not only make mothers available to the work force, but also limit the exposure that children have to the family environment. New nations frequently find that extended familial (tribal) ties are the chief obstacles to acceptance of the new political order. Perhaps the antifamily posture of some contem-

78

porary radical thought is based in part on a perceived danger of perpetuating political conservatism.

Thus, as an agent of socialization, the family is almost universally either prized or despised. An institution that is attributed so much power by both its friends and its enemies must have something going for it. Accordingly, we should subject it to some scrutiny.

Although the family probably functions primarily as a conservatizing influence, one of the most intriguing findings on the family is that it can operate to communicate unorthodox political norms as well. Interview data from Russian emigrants was expected to reveal that parents who had grown up prior to the revolution would, in the early days of the new Soviet regime, be very conservative socializing influences on their children. Government officials anticipated just such a family interference with their own socialization program. However, these parents, despite the fact that they did not particularly believe in or admire the principles of the new revolutionary government, tried to make their children into good Soviet citizens. Instead of subverting the regime, they were doing its socialization for it.[1] Of course, this is not really so strange. These Russian parents were apparently attempting to provide their offspring with skills and values that would enable them to succeed in their environment; such paradoxical socialization was rational indeed. Rather than impeding social change, this older generation was helping to make it more widely accepted.

Thus, as we begin to investigate the processes by which the parental family may impart political signals to the young, we should keep in mind that the end result of the process is not simply to promote the past. The total effect may be considerably more subtle than that.

THE PROCESSES OF PARENTAL SOCIALIZATION

The major goal of this chapter is to determine how much substance there is in the ancient expectation, "like father, like son." How much of children's political orientation can be explained in terms of transmissions from their parents? Further, if there *is* parent-to-child influence, what is the process by which this influence is communicated? There seem to be at least three identifiable processes that might be involved. Two of them, as we shall see, are quite indirect.

The Circumstances of Birth. Much of what happens to a person throughout his lifetime is a consequence of the conditions into which he happened to be born. Some of these conditions undoubtedly have consequences for mass political behavior. For example, a child grows up in working-class environment because he happens to be born to working-class parents. As a consequence, he is likely to live in certain kinds of neighborhoods, attend some schools rather than others, and have rather different kinds of associates than his counterpart in the middle class. Any of these factors may be the source of important political stimuli. Moreover, despite the possibility of mobility, a child born into the working class is likely to remain in that class all his life. Thus, in one sense his objective political interests are determined by the circumstances of his birth.[2] Other circumstances of birth—such as ethnic group status or race—may have similar consequences.

Of course, one could argue that this process is not family political socialization at all, for it does not depend on anything that the parents may do to the child. What it does suggest is that exposure to certain kinds of political influences is likely to be determined by very early and family-related circumstances. A more complete explanation of this process requires an understanding of the socialization effects of other agents and a knowledge of how class, ethnic groups, and so on, affect political behavior. However, this stage-setting function of family ought not to be disregarded by the student of socialization, for it does illustrate the importance of a youthful period in explaining political orientations, and it does indicate how the impacts of diverse agents may be subtly related.

Direct Value Transfer. The most obvious hypothesis about the influence of parents upon their children is simply that parents teach their preferred values and that youngsters learn them. Certainly children must learn a great deal from their parents. It is impossible for youngsters to grow up uninfluenced by those around them. The infant acquires most of the characteristics we associate with the human child and then with the human adult through the process of learning. Surprisingly little "humanness" is biologically inherited. Children learn to make their needs for food and other necessities known and eventually to speak in response to the reactions of "significant others." Significant others dispense rewards and impose punishments. In this way, the more or less random responses of the infant acquire meaning. Certain of these movements or actions result in rewards from the significant others while some are ignored or punished. The infant learns to repeat the gratification-eliciting acts and to refrain from others. Thus, the child learns to do what is effective in his environment; he learns to conform; he learns to become a human being. Conformity, then, at least in very basic things, is an important part of early childhood. Leaving a child alone to "do his own thing" is impossible, for the only way he can have an "own thing" to do is by learning it. All other sources of social behavior—such as divine or mystic implantation—seem unlikely given present evidence.

Of course, chief among the early significant others are parents, whose dominance of all aspects of the young child's life is enormous, as is their nearly exclusive role in providing food, protection, and affection. This much is obvious. The really interesting question is whether there are any political norms to which the child is urged to conform. Evidence is that indeed there are. First, families undoubtedly transmit culturally defined values of a rather general nature; that is, there may be non-political learning which has political consequences. An interesting example—and one which has contemporary significance—concerns the status of women. As noted in chapter 2, there is no question that in our society women still occupy a somewhat passive role. They are less aggressive, less participatory, and less interested in things outside the home. Whether or not one likes this, it is, at the moment, a fact of life, and one, moreover, that is not entirely dependent on objective constraints such as those surrounding childbearing, for both men and women *believe* that this is a proper state of affairs. In considerable measure, women are retiring because they believe they should be retiring. Thus, we are faced with a consequence of socialization. How are people brought to believe that this is the proper state of affairs? Undoubtedly the family is heavily involved. Girl children are encouraged to engage in role-appropriate play. They raise children (dolls), play house, and otherwise mimic domestic activities. This kind of activity is approved and rewarded by parents, while boys are encouraged to play at more active, professional, and leadership roles.

Not surprisingly, this role differentiation has some political concomitants. Women—and this is particularly true at the working-class level—are far less participatory than men. They are more locally oriented and in general less sophisticated.[3] Again, this could be a consequence of some objective condition or even of direct discrimination by men. But at least in part it is because different political roles have been learned, and this learning clearly extends back into early childhood. Even as early as the fourth grade, boys are better informed about politics, more attuned to the possibility of political change, and more willing to evaluate political figures.[4] Admittedly, there is some evidence that the specific imperative, "politics is not for girls," does come to be appreciated at a very young age (apparently learned from observation of male political dominance in the typical American family), but it is likely that a more potent determinant of early sex differentiation in politics stems from more general socialization. From the beginning, boys are encouraged to be aggressive and outgoing, while girls are taught to be domestic and concerned with personal relations. The congruence of the former with the conflict-ridden character of politics is obvious—and probably weighty in its implications.

Of course, families transmit other cultural norms as well. It is likely that some of them also have political implications. Early religious instruction is probably mostly the province of parents, and it is entirely possible that the possession of religious beliefs has some impact on community-supportive values. In chapter 2, we saw that community and religious objects were often confused by the child. Teaching the child to revere God may inadvertently urge him to revere the polity.

Although such transmission may be of considerable significance, the role of the family as a direct communicator of values is not limited to such general themes. Specifically political communication may occur as well. Parents do appear to provide political norms—sometimes consciously, sometimes not—for their offspring.

There is relatively little hard evidence on the impact of family teaching on children's attitudes toward the political community or on affect toward symbols and values of the regime. Part of the reason for this is that in America, where most research of this type has been carried out, such orientations are highly consensual. It is difficult to locate children with relatively negative orientations and then determine whether their socialization experiences have differed. Second, it is difficult to obtain information on what a given child's parents have sought to communicate to him about community or regime. Establishing parental inputs is always difficult, but questions of patriotism and loyalty represent an especially sensitive area of inquiry about parent-child relations. Nonetheless, many scholars believe that parents typically do present only "the conventional ideals about political authority rather than about known or suspected grimmer realities," to their children and that this results in direct absorption of positive attitudes.[5]

In addition, there is other evidence that parents are partly responsible for their children's political orientations toward the community. There are some, though not especially great, differences in the way children are oriented toward *compliance to the law* according to their social class. Lower-class children are more inflexible about the law, more unquestioning about obedience, and more convinced of legal fairness. This greater degree of lower-class support for the established order has been noted among adults and is visible in many ways today—not the least of which is the level of working-class support for the Vietnam war. Since child-rearing practices with regard to response to rules and regulations are known to vary by social class, it is reasonable to attribute these childhood class effects on compliance to the laws as stemming from differential treatment by parents.[6] Very likely, what parents specifically tell their children about the laws produces a visible effect.

A recent study of Appalachia showed that in fatherless homes children were more likely to have positive orientations toward figures of the regime, particularly the President. The most likely explanation for this hinges on three propositions. First, it is probably the case that the prevailing subcultural values of this area are considerably more antiregime than in most parts of the country. Second, it is likely that parents hold and communicate these more antiregime feelings to their children. Third, in those homes that are fatherless, the family unit has lost a powerful political communicator (remember the findings on male political dominance) and is less efficient in promoting antiregime views. These children, accordingly, emerge relatively more proregime than their counterparts with two parents. If this is the case, then it is reasonable to regard the parental family as an important direct teacher of regime-level values.[7]

Finally, as was discussed in chapter 3, studies of political protest by college youth reveal that demonstrators frequently seem to be acting out the political ideals that their parents held but never expressed in actual behavior. To be sure, this does not mean that the clearly antiregime behavior of young people is underlaid by antiregime principles of the older generation; the ideals of the older generation need not have had an antiregime imperative at all; they may have focused on peace or racial equality. It may be only in the attempt of their children to fulfill them that this dimension is realized. Nonetheless, it is probably true that the protest behavior would not have occurred except for parental teaching of specific political values. The role of the parent, though a one-to-one correspondence in principle and action is not involved, seems undeniable.

Direct family learning of regime-level participatory values is also a reality of current politics, if not an overwhelmingly powerful principle. Several studies of voting behavior in adults suggest that participation in elections is related to having been raised in a home where political discussion and political activity were present. That is, active adults can recall similar activity in their home when they were children.[8] It is quite reasonable to believe that childhood transmission of the participatory imperative is responsible for this. Although asking people to recall the conditions of their childhood is somewhat questionable (people may forget their childhood, or inadvertently project their present orientations onto their memories of their parents), this suggestion is bolstered by data on fifth and eighth grade children, which show modest relationships between children's concern for politics and reported levels of parental interest.[9] Further, a study of high school seniors and their parents (involving independent interviews with both) demonstrated that youngsters' political cynicism, an orientation importantly linked to political participation, was slightly related to cynicism in the older generation. However, this holds only for those homes in which there was a great deal of political discussion.[10] Finally, college student data, again depending on recall of parental orientations, show that both political interest in general and participation in student demonstrations are dependent upon the amount of political discussion that characterized the home during childhood. Although these relationships are quite strong, they hold, curiously, only for men students. Perhaps, "men students tend to get their politics from home while the women students get theirs from the campus (or perhaps from the men students)." [11]

While we must conclude that the influence of parents on participatory norms is somewhat limited, we find a different pattern when we inquire whether there is direct transfer of government-level values. In some areas, transfer is apparently very great while in others it is virtually nonexistent. For example, party identification—rare among substantive political values—appears to be well learned from parents. Given the fact that party identification is so critical in people's organizing of politics they experience, it is not surprising that it is developed early. Party identification is a simple and useful device in the interpretation of political stimuli. Perhaps the earliness of acquisition of this orientation accounts for the parents' primary role.

Adult recall data has demonstrated for many years that there is a considerable correspondence between parents and children in the party identification that they hold.[12] This relationship has been found in several countries as well as in the United States. In fact, in nations where party identification does not appear to be very prominent among voters, there is evidence of absence of parent-child political communication.[13] This finding has been confirmed in interview data with very young children (who often attribute a given party identification to the family unit as a whole),[14] and in survey data on Japanese adults and their teen-aged children.[15] The latter result is perhaps the most surprising, given the dramatic social change that nation has experienced in the last century and particularly within the last twenty years.

Although direct value transfer from parent to child occurs, it is doubtful that a conscious indoctrination program is involved. For one thing, the extent of parent-child correspondence in party identification depends upon the amount of control that parents try to exercise over their children. But the relationship here is "curvilinear." That is, a graphed line showing the relationship would first rise and then fall, describing a curve. The most permissive parents are not very successful at inducing their children to imitate their party. Moderately permissive parents are much more successful, while nonpermissive parents again fail, showing a pattern of child correspondence very similar to that of the most permissive parents.[16] Apparently, relative noncommunication about politics does not encourage children to imitate parents, but extreme insistence on political partisan conformity has a backfire effect and does not produce conformity either. Conscious indoctrination is apparently not the mechanism by which intergenerational transmission of party identification proceeds.

A second kind of evidence reinforces the suggestion that transmission proceeds by a less overt process. This involves the relative influence of mothers and fathers. In most cases (74 per cent), both parents in a family profess the same party identification. Under these conditions, it is difficult to say whether a child accepts (or fails to accept) the party identification of one parent as opposed to the other. Either the family norm is transmitted, or it is not. In the case of mother-father division, however, one has an opportunity to observe whether children are more likely to follow mothers or fathers. Although our previously reported findings about male political dominance in the family might lead us to expect that the father's opinions would be preferred, it is, in fact, the mother who has greater influence. Among partisan-heterogeneous parents, the cross-pressures tend to produce independent children (28 per cent), but among the remainder, the mother is preferred by a margin of 40 to 32 per cent.[17] Similarly, in situations where one parent is independent and the other partisan, mothers show greater ability to induce imitation by their children. These findings, incidentally, are found for both boys and girls and prevail in several countries.

This is not really contrary to the evidence of male dominance in the family. It is still the case that youngsters believe in male specialization in politics—both boys and girls indicate that fathers are preferred sources of overt political advice, for example.[18] But acquisition of party identification is probably much more subtle than receiving of advice. Many believe that the superior position of the mother on this dimension is simply a function of the fact that children are typically closer to their mothers and are exposed to them for greater periods of time during their young lives.[19] Subtle communication between mother and child appears to be a great transmitter of party identification across generations. Further, a mother who perseveres in her premarriage party affiliation despite a contrary spouse must be a very staunch and therefore very communicative partisan indeed.

However, the parent-child transmission process seems much weaker when we move from party identification to other government-level values. Issue positions and evaluations of politically relevant groups are less well communicated than party identification. This is perhaps not surprising, for we know from surveys of adults that issue positions are weakly held and very unstable over time. People are simply not keenly attuned to most public issues and are often completely unconcerned about or ignorant of them. Accordingly, issues are typically very weak criteria for making voting decisions, and issue awareness does little to structure most people's orientations toward politics. If issues are not salient, it is likely that parents emit few signals about public policy questions, and consequently their children cannot learn much from them.

What influence parents do have on their children's issue positions is confined to very concrete current questions; whether there should be prayers in U.S. public schools; or, in Japan, whether there should be a U.S.–Japanese mutual security treaty.

On more remote and abstract questions—like principles of civil liberties—the degree of agreement drops to nearly nothing. The more visible and immediate a political object is, the more success parents will have in communicating preferred norms to their children about it.

Direct parental teaching, then, appears to be very important in political socialization. However, it is obvious that children are by no means made into carbon copies of their parents. In fact, the transmission process is incomplete with respect to all the objects of socialization. Though parents may be primarily conservatizing agents of political socialization, there is obviously enough slack in learning to allow for considerable change.

The Political Consequences of Family Characteristics: Socialization Without Teaching. Because of their dominant position in the early life of their children, parents no doubt have an impact in ways other than through specific teaching. Parents shape children in many ways and are primarily responsible for the determination of the personalities of their children. They establish patterns of decision making and ways of interacting with the outside world. Parental behavior patterns become a standard or norm against which much that the child subsequently encounters can be evaluated. In short, many general features of the child's life-style are determined in the parental environment. It is possible, of course, that some of these general features, though themselves devoid of any specific political content, have political implications for the child.

Let us first consider the matter of personality development. The question of what personality is has been debated vigorously for many years. At this point, let us be content to say that personality refers to internalized mental characteristics of human beings. In one sense, any mind-related feature, including opinions and particular preferences, could be considered personality. But it seems advantageous to be slightly more restrictive and refer to personality as identifiable general dispositions that are relatively enduring. We often say that a person has a pleasing personality if he is generally disposed to be happy, smiling, and friendly; similarly, a person who has a general disposition to be truculent, aggressive, and scornful we dismiss as having an unpleasant personality. In general, we think of these kinds of personalities as relatively unchanging.

The interesting question, of course, is whether there are any political behavior consequences of having particular kinds of personality dispositions. It is reasonable to think that there might be. For example, a person who has a "good" personality, as defined above, would be much more likely to seek an elite role in politics than one with a "bad" personality. Success in such a role involves interaction with, and approval of, other people. Thus, though personality is too general to have any specifically political components, it may well have political behavior implications.

On the mass level, one particular personality characteristic has attracted the attention of many political scientists. This is authoritarianism. Persons defined as authoritarian are likely to structure all situations involving interpersonal relations in terms of rigid status hierarchies, that is, authority relations. The authoritarian interprets his own role as one of submission to those perceived as higher in status and of dominance over those perceived to be lower. A preoccupation with propriety, established orders, and constraint by rules and regulations characterizes this personality type.

An immediate guess would be that authoritarian personality might have important relationships to regime-level orientations. There is considerable evidence that it does. Noncriticism of political authority,[20] certain kinds of deviancy in political views,[21] and attraction to right-wing groups have been found to correlate with authoritarianism in adults,[22] while a tendency to attribute greater power to political figures has been observed in authoritarian children.[23] If, as most psychologists believe, personality is heavily influenced by early experiences within the family, such findings become interesting to the student of political socialization. For example, authoritarianism is found to result from rigid child-rearing patterns. Both recall data from adults and direct studies of children reveal this to be the case.[24] Political scientists, too, have indicated a large parental role in the development of authoritarianism. Lane believes that impaired father relationships lead to authoritarian outlooks. This impairment might result from lack of affection, extreme punitiveness, rejection, or some other distressing relationship.[25] Langton found that Jamaican male students from father-absent families were more authoritarian than those from complete families. This finding, which does not hold for females, is probably due to the fact that males who do not have the security of identification with a same-sex parent become somewhat inflexible in their beliefs.[26] Jaros showed that degree of parental punitiveness, that is, the severity of punishment that parents apply in disciplining children, is related to authoritarianism in grade school children.[27]

Thus, parental practices, though they may be completely unpolitical and have no political motivation, may have profound impact on political behavior of children. Political effects of personality characteristics other than authoritarianism—for example, self-esteem—have also been isolated.

A second kind of unintentional parental socialization is one that has been discussed since ancient times. It is conceivable that children's experiences with, and emotional reactions to, authority figures in their immediate environment (again, typically the parents) are somehow transferred to more remote authority figures (including political ones). In chapter 1, we saw that Confucius believed that love for the prince was an extension of "filial piety." Political loyalty is thought to be a reflection of parental loyalty. For children, the regime is but family writ large.[28]

Some of the first socialization research was predicated, in part, on this venerable hypothesis. It showed that most children indeed do have very positive images of their fathers and simultaneously hold very positive images of political figures, notably the President. This similarity of image suggests that there might be a relationship.[29] However, actual attempts to determine whether children with relatively poor relationships with their father develop relatively negative images of political authority and vice versa have produced little or no support for this transfer notion. An Appalachian study found impaired family situations did not result in less regard for political figures.[30] Although a national survey of grade school children reports that "the child who has a strong father tends to be more attached to figures and institutions of the political system, particularly the President and the policeman, than the child whose father is relatively weak," [31] it also must conclude that "non-family political figures are viewed as considerably more similar to each other than they are viewed as similar to family figures." [32]

A variant of the transfer hypothesis has to do with anxiety. Some argue that young children perceive their parents to be superpowerful, since they are the clear source of all gratifications and punishments in early life. Being confronted with a superbeing of this kind is highly anxiety-arousing, for such a being has tremendous destructive potential, goes the argument. Since the child possesses no resources with which to propitiate such a superpower, he must believe it to be good, benevolent, serving, and kind. Entertaining the possibility that the parental super-power might have malevolent intent would produce intolerable anxiety. Therefore, children love their parents and hold elevated images of them. Supposedly, the child becomes aware of even greater superpowers in the form of political authority. This causes a return of the familiar anxiety. The response is similar; the child reacts to the supreme power of political figures in the same way that he reacted to parental power—he elevates it and loves it to avoid the anxiety of contemplating its hurtful potential. Children literally must love both parent and President.

Although this argument has a dramatic ring to it, there is little evidence that it is valid. Research on children demonstrates no relationship between anxiety level and the extent to which political figures are evaluated positively.[33] Despite the fact that family authority orientations may have implications for childhood socialization, it is quite unlikely that a direct transfer of something like a "father image" to a political figure takes place. Attributing the success of a political candidate to his appeal as a father figure for voters has been popular, but before we can accept the occurrence of a significant transfer of affect from the parental environment to the political environment, much more convincing evidence will have to be accumulated.

Finally, it is possible that certain characteristics of the family result in particular child political orientations through processes less pervasive than personality development and less overt than authority orientation transfer. This kind of parental political socialization is a mixed, miscellaneous category, dependent on the fact that children respond in predictable ways to many characteristics of their families. Family practices thus can affect learning situations, can create various patterns of expectations, and can provide different opportunities for identification. We must look at a few of the possible political consequences of such contingencies within the parental family.

Almond and Verba surveyed adult citizens in five nations and revealed some interesting data about the extent to which people could recall ability to participate in family decisions. In all five countries, those who had some impact on family decisions as adolescents displayed higher levels of regime-level participatory values than those who did not have such influence. They felt much more competent to influence government decisions.[34] Such values, of course, influence actual participation and are probably important for the presence or absence of democratic government. Apparently, such family participation enables youngsters to gain confidence in their own efforts, to acquire a sense of competence. In other words, they learn that participatory efforts bring results. The transfer of this learning to the political realm appears to occur without much difficulty.

Pinner, in a comparative study, wondered why Belgian and French students displayed more political distrust than their Dutch counterparts. It appeared that the Belgian and French cultures emphasize more parental overprotection of the young than does Dutch culture. Pinner showed that these two observations are related; overprotected youth—regardless of their nationality—tend to be more distrustful of political figures and institutions.[35] Of course, the implications for both government- and regime-level political support are obvious. Supposedly, this is because inherent in overprotection of a child is the creation of the expectation that the outside world is threatening. Thus, "where young people experience much parental overprotection the transition from the warm protection of the home into the world at large—of which politics is part—is viewed with fear and apprehension. Consequently, youngsters so overprotected will demonstrate political distrust and political disaffection." [36]

Finally, let us consider children's ability to identify with parents. We saw earlier that not having the security of same-sex parental identification was likely to produce certain effects in Jamaican boys' personalities. This lack of identification may well have some less extensive but nonetheless politically relevant consequences as well. Lack of identification with a male figure may inhibit the taking of sex-appropriate roles. Thus, given male political dominance, fatherless boys should be less politically interested and less participatory than their two-parent counterparts. In fact, it was discovered that two regime-level participatory values, political interest and political efficacy, were impaired in boys from fatherless families.

Moreover, the family characteristic need not be so overt as an absent father. If the father is dominated by the mother, his weak presence is also reflected in diminished participatory norms as well as in diminished actual political participation in his male offspring.[37] Family circumstances which deprive children of—or even just weaken—figures with which to identify can thus have considerable political socializational consequences.

Undoubtedly, there are other aspects of the family environment which can produce political responses. Many of them are unknown right now. But in any event, we should be aware that parents, by their most innocent acts, may be inadvertently socializing their children to politics and, indeed, probably could not stop molding their children even if they wanted to. They cannot avoid shaping their personalities, they cannot avoid providing an authority structure, and they cannot avoid providing a multitude of salient features in the family environment. Perhaps this completely unintentional socialization is just as significant in the long run as specific parental political indoctrination.

THE IMPACT OF THE FAMILY

Is family the great conservator of political stability? Is it the major impediment to political change? These ancient questions, we have seen, are somewhat incorrectly formulated. Even though the family may be influential, it is not necessarily the case that only traditional values may be communicated. Indeed, families can aid in the consolidation of change by helping to communicate the new orthodoxy rather than the old.

Over and above this is the question of whether families can communicate their preferred political values to the child, whatever the nature of those values. It is clear that the answer is at least partly in the affirmative. This is considerable but hardly definitive evidence that a great deal of transfer goes on. But it is also clear that children are not fully chips off the old political block. As we move away from general cultural orientations or obvious and overt variables like party identification to specific issue preferences or abstract notions, the influence of family declines. Further, there is some evidence that if parents try to indoctrinate children in their own values, they may well fail to communicate anything. Learning parental political values is not typically an overt process.

The fact that much inadvertent socialization may proceed from the family (as we have just seen) reinforces our view that the family, while clearly important, is definitely not a one-to-one transfer device. The family exerts a complex of influences on the child, and many of them are not recognizable as specifically political influences. The socialized child who emerges, therefore, may be quite different from his parents. This is not so strange, for parents may be politically socializing their children without even knowing it. Family influence is very subtle and many faceted. We must agree that the family is an effective political socializer, but we must always ask, How is it effective, and effective toward what? The assertion that the family directly protects old, established values is clearly an oversimplification based on incomplete understanding.

NOTES

1. Alex Inkeles, "Social Change and Social Character: The Role of Parental Mediation," *Journal of Social Issues*, 11 (May 1955): 12–23.
2. Robert E. Lane, *Political Ideology* (New York: Free Press, 1962), chap. 17; Richard E. Dawson and Kenneth Prewitt, *Political Socialization* (Boston: Little, Brown & Co., 1969), chap. 7.
3. See, e.g., M. Kent Jennings and Richard G. Niemi, "The Division of Labor Between Mothers and Fathers," *American Political Science Review*, 65 (March 1971): 69–82.
4. Fred I. Greenstein, *Children and Politics* (New Haven: Yale University Press, 1965), pp. 115–18.
5. David Easton and Jack Dennis, *Children in the Political System* (New York: McGraw-Hill Book Co., 1969), p. 358.

6. Robert D. Hess and Judith V. Torney, *The Development of Political Attitudes in Children* (Chicago: Aldine Publishing Co., 1967), pp. 137–44.
7. Dean Jaros et al., "The Malevolent Leader: Political Socialization in an American Sub-culture," *American Political Science Review*, 62 (June 1968): 564–75.
8. Lester W. Milbrath, *Political Participation* (Chicago: Rand McNally & Co., 1965), p. 43.
9. Charles F. Andrain, *Children and Civic Awareness* (Columbus, Ohio: Charles E. Merrill Publishing Co., 1971), p. 143.
10. M. Kent Jennings and Richard G. Niemi, "The Transmission of Political Values from Parent to Child," *American Political Science Review*, 62 (March 1968): 169–84.
11. J. Leiper Freeman, "Parents, It's Not All Your Fault, But . . . .," *Journal of Politics*, 31 (August 1969): 816.
12. Angus Campbell et al., *The American Voter* (New York: John Wiley & Sons, 1960), pp. 146–49; Herbert McCloskey and Harold Dahlgren, "Primary Group Influence on Party Loyalty," *American Political Science Review*, 53 (September 1959): 762–70.
13. Philip Converse and Georges Dupuex, "Politicization of the Electorate in France and the United States," *Public Opinion Quarterly*, 26 (Spring 1962): 23–30.
14. Greenstein, *op. cit.*, pp. 74–78.
15. Akira Kubota and Robert E. Ward, "Family Influence and Political Socialization in Japan," *Comparative Political Studies*, 3 (July 1970): 140–75.
16. Eleanor E. Maccoby et al., "Youth and Political Change," *Public Opinion Quarterly*, 18 (Spring 1954): 23–39.
17. Kenneth P. Langton, *Political Socialization* (New York: Oxford University Press, 1969), pp. 52–83.
18. Greenstein, *op. cit.*, p. 119.
19. Langton, *loc. cit.*; Kubota and Ward, *op. cit.*
20. Lane, *op. cit.*
21. Giuseppe DiPalma and Herbert McCloskey, "Personality and Conformity: The Learning of Political Attitudes," *American Political Science Review*, 64 (December 1970): 1054–73.
22. Ira S. Rohter, "Social and Psychological Determinants of Radical Rightism," in *The American Right Wing*, Robert A. Schoenberger, ed. (New York: Holt, Rinehart & Winston, 1969), pp. 193–238.
23. Dean Jaros, "Children's Orientations Toward the President: Some Additional Theoretical Considerations and Data," *Journal of Politics*, 29 (May 1967): 368–87.
24. Fred I. Greenstein, *Personality and Politics* (Chicago: Markham Publishing Co., 1969), pp. 110–14.
25. Lane, *op. cit.*
26. Langton, *op. cit.*, pp. 32, 40.
27. Jaros, *loc. cit.*
28. Sebastian Degrazia, *The Political Community* (Chicago: University of Chicago Press, 1948), chap. 1.
29. Robert D. Hess and David Easton, "The Child's Changing Image of the President," *Public Opinion Quarterly*, 24 (Winter 1960): 632–44.
30. Jaros, et al., *op. cit.*
31. Hess and Torney, *op. cit.*, p. 101.
32. *Ibid.*, p. 100.
33. Jaros, *op. cit.*

34. Gabriel Almond and Sidney Verba, *The Civic Culture* (Boston: Little, Brown & Co., 1965), pp. 284–87.
35. Frank A. Pinner, "Parental Overprotection and Political Distrust," *The Annals*, 361 (September 1965): 58–70.
36. *Ibid.*, p. 60.
37. Langton, *op. cit.*, chap. 2.

5. The Socializers:
School and College

While almost all scholars of political socialization have given much attention to the family, political activists of all types, from extreme apologists for the status quo to wild-eyed revolutionaries, have devoted the bulk of their thinking to a different socialization agent—the school. Civic education, we have seen, has been a prominent feature of all regimes since ancient times, and formal educational processes and schools are subject to manipulation as a matter of policy. In many nations—for example, the Soviet Union and France—a national curriculum is imposed. Political leaders can heavily influence what is taught about politics in the school, whereas their control over the family or other institutions is likely to be marginal, at best. Hence, the most direct way that political power holders can influence the process of political socialization in their own behalf is by determining the political content of the formal education of the young and choosing those who teach it. Would-be power holders have dreamed of manipulating the schools; actual power holders have done it.

Citizens, as well as leaders, respond to the apparent manipulability of the schools. Often this takes the form of controversy over what political values are being transmitted by the schools or over who is doing the transmitting. One hears bitter complaints that the schools are failing to transmit the political traditions on which the country is based or, alternatively, are perpetuating a stagnant political orthodoxy. In recent years, many groups have demanded that certain teachers or college professors be fired;

conservatives insist that "controversial" educators—those who too closely question government policy—be dismissed, while liberals find that inadequate sensitivity to minority groups renders a teacher unfit. Disputes over loyalty oaths for teachers and questions about the political reliability of textbook authors crop up periodically to remind us that the school as socialization agent can be a hot political issue.

The tremendous concern over who runs the schools seems to be based on two widely shared assumptions: first, that the schools do in fact exert tremendous political influence on children; and second, that these influence processes are subject to some kind of deliberate control. Of course, these assumptions seem eminently reasonable. For one thing, it is conventional wisdom that democracy requires an educated citizenry. It is easy to assume that the prevailing educational system has been instrumental in bringing about and maintaining the arrangements for political democracy in this country. Further, tremendous commitment of human and fiscal resources for teacher training, curriculum design, instructional materials, and even school physical plants has been made to civic education programs in the United States. For many, the prospect that all this may not be producing profound and beneficent impact on the youth of America is unthinkable. And yet, in point of fact, there is astonishingly little hard evidence that schools really are important agents of political socialization. Since schools occupy a large proportion of the attention of individuals during a period of their lives when they acquire many enduring dispositions, they clearly have great potential as political indoctrinators; but how much actual influence they have is another, and largely unknown, matter.

These remarks suggest that there are two broad kinds of questions about the schools that students of political socialization should ask. On the one hand, there is the *cognitive and value output* of the schools. What are the schools communicating in the way of information and preferred values, and to what extent, if at all, do these communications have an impact on their recipients? Since there are many possible ways in which schools could influence their students, we ought to investigate alternative socialization processes that might be operative.

However, there is a second great concern, which, though it could also be relevant to all agents of political socialization, is particularly applicable to the schools. This is the question of *value input*. Unlike most other agents, schools are specifically designed to communicate political values to the young, if only the reaffirmation of consensual community-level values. Schools represent deliberate, conscious attempts of society to socialize its young. Accordingly, we should ask how schools come to transmit given political values or select given information for communication to the young. By what processes do other institutions of society—the ones that have influence on the schools—induce those educational establishments to reflect preferred political dogma to the young? This chapter will consider several output processes and several input processes and attempt to assess the importance of each toward making the schools significant agents of political socialization.

OUTPUT PROCESSES

Despite the general lack of evidence about the schools' role as socializers, some research suggests that output processes may be operating in education. It is well established that the more education a person receives, the more distinctive his orientations and values. We know that in Western cultures educated people are likely to participate more in conventional politics, to know more about politics, and to hold more regime-level participatory values than their less schooled counterparts.[1] This could mean that something in the school experience stimulates people to participate; schools may socialize participatory values. Other regime-level values thought to be supportive of democracy—libertarianism and willingness to tolerate change—also appear to be characteristic of better-educated citizens.[2] Again, schools in the West may socialize such values. But this evidence does not prove the point. It is entirely possible that persons who for some other reason have become interested in political participation or who have developed libertarian views manage to seek out and acquire more education than those who have not. Education itself may not necessarily cause these characteristic political values.

But even if education does produce these effects, such findings only whet the appetite. What other kinds of political values might be affected by formal education? Remembering chapter 2, we know that many kinds of political orientation deserve our attention. More importantly, perhaps, finding that education and participation are related does nothing to enlighten us about the mechanisms by which education may operate. Exactly what educational experiences encourage these developments? Such incomplete findings only underscore the necessity of exploring alternate processes. We will posit and examine six major processes by which basic political orientations may be communicated by the educational system.[3]

As was the case for family socialization processes, these divide into two basic types: five are direct value-transfer processes, while one, classroom milieu, involves consequences of the nonpolitical features of the educational environment. By direct value transfer, pupils may acquire political orientations through: (1) curricular content alone, (2) curricular content mediated by educational quality, (3) teachers' overt expression of their own values in classroom situations, (4) teachers' more casual expression of their own values in less structured, out-of-class situations, and (5) pupil identification with particular teachers and adoption of values these teachers are perceived to hold. While these processes are discussed individually here, there is nothing mutually exclusive about them. Clearly, more than one may operate simultaneously.

Curricular Content. The belief that curricular content is important to the development of basic political values is widespread. Indeed, much of the public controversy over school control centers around determination of the curriculum. Disputes over course offerings (e.g., should there be a course in black studies) are perhaps the most pointed.

Professional educators, too, perceive a relationship between curricular content and childhood political values. Concerned about how best to prepare youngsters to cope with increasingly complex political life, they have, in the last several years, implemented instructional programs that emphasize many kinds of participation: gathering and evaluating information, involvement in civic affairs, and the exercise of one's rights. Also, there has been some concern with regime-level substantive values, in that the social-conflict-solving nature of politics is stressed along with the virtues of a relatively libertarian political outlook.[4] Unfortunately, the quantity of systematic data about the supposed greater effectiveness of new social studies curriculums is small and the findings are inconclusive in demonstrating the superiority of particular content patterns.[5]

Even more disquieting, the evidence that social studies courses, whatever their nature, have an important impact on the political orientations of children is at best mixed. Several authors show that some substantive values (e.g., extreme ethnocentric patriotism) can be changed as a consequence of exposure to social studies courses, but participatory values do not appear to be subject to the same influence.[6] But many other studies are unable to demonstrate that social studies courses have a discernible impact of any kind (even with respect to increasing levels of information).[7] The most extensive of these studies, using a sample of high school students and their teachers, was so discouraging that the authors comment, "Indeed, the increments are so minuscule as to raise serious questions about the utility of investing in government courses at the high school level." [8] This study found no substantial differences in possession of information among students who had two social studies courses, those with only one, and those with none at all.

The latter study does not imply that courses are inherently incapable of influencing students, however. The authors attribute the lack of impact to the fact that social studies courses are in general bland and characterized by content that students already know. This view is supported by the finding that among black students—who probably suffered from inferior education before getting to high school—some effects could indeed be traced to the high school civics curriculum. For those who had been given only mediocre early training, the course content was new and had an impact. If school curriculums could be made stimulating to larger numbers of people, we might in the future have to modify the general conclusion that any effect of the formal educational process on political socialization is not due to prescribed content alone.

Curricular Content Mediated by Educational Quality. It is possible that curriculums are important, but that their impact may depend on how skillfully and effectively they are transmitted to the pupils. In short, educational quality—the effectiveness of teachers, the level of community investment in up-to-date books and other educational materials, and so on—may determine whether curriculums succeed or fail. Many scholars whose chief concern is curriculum or text content seem to be concerned that teachers' unenlightened and old-fashioned classroom behavior may nullify the anticipated benefits of superior programs.[9]

Teacher capability is regarded as a key variable by nearly all commentators on any kind of educational experience. It seems perfectly obvious that some teachers are effective while others are not. However, the evidence on this point is, again, not definitive from the standpoint of one interested in political socialization. Generally, it is asserted that such teacher qualities as "warmth," "stimulation," "organization," and "responsibility" lead to greater ability to communicate information, provoke thinking, and affect the values of the students.[10] But there are obvious problems in measuring these teacher qualities. How do you know that one teacher is warm and another not? Different children might consider the same teacher "cold," "tepid," and "warm." Moreover, few studies directly determine effectiveness by examining substantive changes induced in pupils. In one bibliography on teacher effectiveness, fewer than 4 per cent of the studies listed relied on this criterion.[11] The usual standard of effectiveness is evaluation of the teacher by principals or other supervisory personnel, other teachers, outside experts, pupils, or the teacher himself.[12] Although this may be fine for some purposes, it is clear that pupil change in information or attitude is the most relevant gauge for evaluating agents of political socialization.

Hence, insofar as political learning is concerned, the role of teacher mediation of curriculum is very much an open question, fully deserving of thorough investigation. The warm, stimulating teacher may be able to produce greater cognitive and attitudinal changes in the political orientations of pupils than his more impersonal and lethargic counterpart. This would mean that any set of values associated with him will be effectively communicated. And, especially in participatory and regime-level substantive realms, curriculums may provide these values.

An intriguing study of the political socialization impacts of educational quality was recently completed by Merelman.[13] Sixth, ninth, and twelfth grade pupils in two school districts, one of high educational quality and one of low, were compared for differences in political information and values. The effects of the differences in educational quality turned out to be "limited but varied." [14] During the last six years of their training, children in the high-quality district absorbed more information about institutional arrangements and political personalities. They also appear to have acquired greater support for the standard symbols of democracy; that is, verbal support for the principle of majority rule or for the activity of voting. However, other regime-level democratic values, such as support for minority rights or, for that matter, motivation to participate, were nearly the same in children of the high-quality district and those of the low-quality district. Looking at some government-level policy preference values, Merelman found that children in the low-quality district were materially lower in support for "domestic liberalism" (social welfare, etc.).

Thus, though its effect is not great, we can say that "quality of education" does have political socialization consequences. Of course, quality of education itself is a complex concept, and we need some information as to just what characteristics of quality education might produce these effects. The high-quality district in the study just discussed had a higher tax rate than its low-quality counterpart, spent more money per pupil on education, and school classes, especially in the higher grades, were much smaller. The availability of more books, libraries, and other facilities and personnel characterized the district, as well. Of course, it is reasonable to expect that high-quality districts would have superior teachers. Indeed, the whole idea of effective teachers mediating curricular content implies that a very significant dimension of educational quality is teacher competence. In fact, Merelman found that social studies teachers in the high-quality district did possess higher qualifications (in terms of degrees, credits, and quality of their colleges), did possess higher morale, and did seem to confront more often the controversy of issues in their teachings.

Could it be, then, that the political socialization differences between the children of these two districts are due to the quality of the respective teachers? Perhaps not, for the differences between the two teaching staffs is not very great. That of the superior district is not greatly distinctive. Though suggestive, the evidence is hardly conclusive.

In summary, there is some reason to believe that curricular content—if it were not redundant or otherwise inherently inferior—could be transmitted to school children under superior educational conditions. But evidence on the topic is quite slim. Especially as far as teacher quality is concerned, we would have expected more convincing results. At least until more comprehensive information is available, we must conclude that the impact of educational quality in general, and teacher effectiveness in particular, is somewhat limited.

Teachers' Overt Expression of Their Own Values in the Classroom. Of course, there are sources of political values other than curriculums to which teachers may respond in communicating with pupils. Most obvious among these are teachers' own attitudes and beliefs, which might be a basis for change induced in pupils regardless of whether or not the teachers agree with anything in the curriculum. It is likely that many teachers hold regime-level substantive values at variance with those that characterize most curriculums. Minority-group teachers, or those who for one reason or another are somewhat critical of authority, might fall into this group. Moreover, virtually all teachers must have attitudinal structures of far greater scope and complexity than could be expressed in the prescriptions of formal educational materials. Most teachers certainly entertain a variety of government-level values about current issues of public policy, while curriculums are generally silent on these topics.[15]

Again, the suggestion that teachers communicate their political values to their pupils is hardly new. Political power holders have routinely assumed that this process takes place, and consequently concern about teachers' political reliability has been common. Professional educators, apparently also believing in this process, deplore the transmission of personal government-level values. Prevailing dogma seems to be that children must be brought to deal "critically" with political issues, but not indoctrinated about them.[16]

Research on the behavior of American teachers, however, suggests that their government-level value role is one of noninvolvement.[17] Most teachers, often abetted by the texts that they use, strike poses of explicit political neutrality. Probably in response to pressure—real or imagined—from influential groups in society, teachers may avoid discussion of all but the most consensual community- and regime-level values. The desire to avoid communicating government-level values is so strong, it is sometimes argued, that teachers even fail to communicate the fact that public policy .involves social conflict and the resolution of different value positions.[18] Whether or not teachers are responsible, we have noted before that youngsters unrealistically do indeed tend to regard politics as a conflictless enterprise.

Thus, the picture of the value role of the teacher is, for the most part, one of overt disinterest. Except where the teacher's values are highly consensual, they seem to be shielded from exposure. Most political values, especially issue values, thus do not seem to enter the classroom through the teacher.

Two caveats modify this general finding, however. First, teachers may indeed communicate their own values on *consensual* regime and community questions. Though teachers may thus be only reaffirming the value of apple pie and motherhood, such learning is indeed important. If teachers socialize by virtue of communicating their personal conventional values, this is a fact of some significance. Indeed, an extensive study of grade school children indicates that as youngsters proceed through their years of schooling, their political values on such matters come increasingly to approximate those of their teachers.[19] It is possible that there is a causal link. Second, teacher values may enter the political socialization process through some sort of latent process, or one more difficult to observe. The next two output processes to be discussed are such.

Value Expression Outside of Class. It is possible that values are transferred from teacher to child during informal contacts outside the classroom context. Teachers feel less constrained in their behavior outside the classroom and might well be willing to embark upon discussions of political matters considered quite inappropriate for the formal, structured setting of the classroom. Not only is this kind of contact likely to result in the exposure of more of the teacher's values, but it is also particularly likely to be effective. Professional educators have long argued that learning is facilitated by the existence of a meaningful personal relationship between teacher and pupil.[20] This kind of personal interaction is typical of the great variety of "extracurricular activities" available to today's youngster, and such relationships are a valuable supplement to the relatively one-sided arrangements that characterize classrooms.[21]

While this process might be operative most often with respect to issue values, there is no reason why regime- or community-level values could not be communicated in the same way. Teachers with unorthodox values would be likely to find this process their most appropriate outlet.

Unfortunately, we cannot say whether political socialization in the schools follows this process or not, for no one has investigated it. However, as we shall soon see, there is some suggestion that nonclass interaction between college students and their instructors encourages the former to adopt the political values of the latter. If teachers do talk about politics to their pupils outside of class —and, we must admit, it is not certain that they do—it is probably the case that values are transmitted. But until more evidence is at hand, we must withhold final judgment.

Teachers as Models for Political Values. Teachers can function as transmitters of political values without any conscious effort on their part. Children may acquire values by a process of identification with teachers rather than as a result of compliance with the imperatives of an overt communication. Children apparently learn not only by the standard reward-punishment process of classical learning theory, but also by observing and reproducing the actions of other individuals, often adults.[22] It is very likely that teachers thus serve as models for some behaviors and attitudes for some children, and it is possible that some of these behaviors and attitudes are political.[23] To be sure, teachers might be difficult to imitate politically since they tend, as a group, to assume political neutrality, at least in the classroom. But teachers may signal their political values in places other than the classroom, as just discussed, or may, in the course of discussing the political materials inherent in the social studies curriculum, emit cues which inadvertently reveal their values to pupils. Although this seems to be a likely process, there are no data at all that can help us to determine whether it really occurs. Our list of questions awaiting further evidence for answers grows.

Participatory and Permissive Classroom Milieu. There remains the question of whether there are operative in the school environment more subtle value acquisition processes, just as in the family setting children may undergo totally nonpolitical experiences that have political socialization consequences. People who can recall having participated in family decisions might have higher levels of political participatory values. Some kind of transfer of a more general belief in participation seems to occur. Is there evidence of a similiar transfer from the school environment? Educators have long insisted that this is in fact the case. A relatively permissive classroom rather than a structured and authoritarian one, an environment in which students participate in the formulations of decisions rather than merely receiving them from an authoritative source, is supposed to contribute to the development of critical, "reflective," and informed citizens.[24] Support for this proposition is mixed, but the most comprehensive studies confirm that adults who recall being able to complain about unfair treatment in school and who recall participating in classroom discussions feel much more competent to engage in democratic political affairs.[25] This finding is reported in several countries.

In a similar vein, it is sometimes suggested that the schools lay excessive emphasis on obedience to rules. Supposedly, this inculcation to following authoritative imperatives has consequences for political obedience as well; children might become robotlike rule-followers rather than active, participatory citizens. However, there is no evidence that stringency of school rules has any implications of later political docility.

INPUT PROCESSES

Though the schools' impact on students seems limited and difficult to assess in all of its ramifications, they are probably effective agents of socialization, at least along some dimensions. The critical remaining question concerns the way in which agents are controlled. This, as we have seen, is a historic question of considerable moment. Of course, control can imply conscious effort on the part of a board of education or some community group to manipulate particular elements of educational content for a given locale. It can also refer to widespread customs or practices, which may or may not be undertaken with the idea of affecting the political output of educational practices.

We have already looked at one kind of conscious, specific control—undertaken quite frequently and openly: determination of text and curricular content. Although its effect seems limited when particular aspects of curriculum are manipulated,[26] it is quite possible that broad, nearly universal features of American school curriculums, dictated by general acceptance of cultural norms, are not without impact. Suppose that the typical American curriculum were replaced with one that advocated an end to nationalism and the establishment of world government. Would such a great change be important? Since such an event has not occurred, it is impossible to say. Nonetheless, curriculum control should not be dismissed out of hand as an input process. Perhaps some comparisons of children in different nations, who have truly experienced extremely different curriculums, would contribute to answering this question.

However, the generally negative findings encourage us to devote most of our attention to input processes that involve teachers. We shall examine three such. (1) Through a process of selective recruitment, persons of particular social backgrounds could be brought to the teaching profession. Having already been "properly" socialized within these background contexts, such persons could be counted on to teach their particular political values. (2) Teacher training could be conducted in such a manner that the values expected to be taught are made clear to new recruits. If training is a meaningful experience, these expectations would be acted upon. (3) Induction to the values of the local community may occur after the teacher has begun work. Such norms may include teaching the political values that are congenial to particular elites and that may be dominant in a given locale.

Background Factors and Selective Recruitment. Undoubtedly, the most prominent finding about the social backgrounds of teachers is that the profession attracts two groups: "the sons of the working class and the daughters of the middle and upper classes." [27] Prior to World War II, teaching was largely the province of middle-class women. It was during this period that the old principle of educational sociology developed: that middle-class values (largely regime-level and issue values) are communicated through the schools because teachers, themselves of the middle class, are representative of those values. With the end of World War II, socially mobile lower-class males began to seek out the teaching profession. Did the introduction of different class backgrounds to the teaching profession notably alter the value output of the schools? The answer appears to be negative.[28] However, we must remember that these working-class males are decidedly mobile. They are acquiring white-collar status, and anticipatory socialization makes it unlikely that these men would often challenge the values of the class to which they aspire. Recruitment patterns with no conscious bias may therefore select teachers who are committed to middle-class values.

Of course, selective recruitment can be used as a conscious and direct control mechanism. We have already seen how politically unreliable teachers are screened out in some regimes, particularly totalitarian ones, and stories of dismissals of teachers with unorthodox political views are common in the United States today. However, this method of controlling political value input to the schools has its limitations. Attempts of a school district to recruit an elite crop of teachers who might possess more democratic political attitudes, communicate more political information, and in general reflect a greater degree of political sensitivity might well fail simply because the desired kinds of teachers are not available in large numbers. One cannot selectively recruit if there is little from which to select.[29]

The recruitment pattern of teachers is in some flux, however. Great changes sweep through our society, affecting the status and chances of different classes and minority groups (including, significantly for any consideration of teachers, women). What teachers are called upon to do (for example, in ghetto areas) and the rewards they receive are changing dramatically. This will affect who is recruited and may well have implications for the political value input to the schools. Social conditions are intimately linked to political education, and current social change promises, through its impact on the recruitment of educators, to produce some dramatic results. It is also clear that conscious selective recruitment can affect value input, but, despite its overt and obvious nature, it is probably limited in its feasibility.

Teacher Training. Teacher training is probably important for the value input to American schools. Many kinds of teacher behavior, from various performance criteria to "expressivism" to preference for textbooks, have been found to depend upon both the kind and amount of training.[30] Not only does this appear to be true for strictly professionally relevant variables, but norms about political expression also appear to be dependent upon college major and kind of degree. Willingness to delve into political controversy or advocate particular political values in the classroom and willingness to personally undertake political activity in the community are both more characteristic of social science majors than education majors and are more likely to be exhibited by master's degree holders than bachelor's degree holders. The former relationship is particularly pronounced.[31] Another piece of evidence about the importance of teacher training input shows that the expression of participatory values depends most heavily on teachers' perceptions of values held by college instructors.[32]

A critical question for value input to the schools is, then, "Who teaches the teachers?" As teachers with greater educational diversity enter the profession, and as colleges of education undergo development and change, becoming intellectually less isolated, a rather different kind of political offering may be made to school children. Students preparing to be teachers are less restricted to course work in stuffy, ingrown education programs; they partake of the more heady atmosphere of academic disciplines. Moreover, education programs themselves seem to be emerging from a closed, independent world. They show increasing appreciation of wider scholarship. While political conventionality may have characterized the norms surrounding the preparation of teachers in the past, this condition cannot be expected to continue in these dynamic times.

On-the-Job Induction. Different kinds of communities have different political cultures. It is possible that teachers, after arriving in communities and becoming aware of the prevailing mores, are somehow brought to communicate appropriate political values. As members of a profession, teachers have been compliant, noncompetitive, and deferential. Strong expectations about the proper political ideas, especially regime-level ideas, and ability to reach the minds of the young often agitate individuals and groups in both public and private positions. Perceiving this, teachers might become quite aware not only of what is expected of them but also of the sanctions that will be imposed for inappropriate behavior.

However, this does not always occur. At least in some areas, and for reasons that are not clear, teachers are profoundly ignorant of the desires of community groups or of their efforts to influence education. Teachers "function in a political vacuum, having neither the knowledge nor the connections necessary to understand decision making in their districts." [33] In general, they are not aware of community agents who affect school policy, nor can they identify groups that support education or oppose it. Is it the case that in these areas community political input to teachers does not exist? Not necessarily, for some sort of unconscious process seems to operate. It is known that political teaching behavior varies greatly with local community characteristics. The region of the country in which a community is located, as well as its urban or rural character, appears to affect its teachers' behavior.[34] Whether by purposive effort or not, communities do produce particular kinds of political inputs to the schools through teachers.

One way that this might be accomplished is through indirect controls. Teachers may feel few external influences, but they are sensitive to internal pressures. Most inducements for conformity emanate from within their professional milieu.[35] It is possible that some of these inducements have political content. It is quite possible that principals or other administrators—who do experience direct community pressures [36]—relay local political imperatives to teachers.

Outputs of, and Inputs to, the Schools. Does the person who controls the schools control the political destiny of the nation? Is the school the supremely manipulable institution, which, through a few declarations of public educational policy, molds the political beings of the young?

With regard to the impact of the schools on the political

orientations of the young, it is clear that schools do in fact socialize. But again, the processes of socialization are complex, and the total influence of the educational system is not as pervasive as one might like to believe. By far the most frequently studied political orientations are regime-level values having to do with democracy, particularly those related to participation. While it is true that quantity of education apparently contributes to the degree to which these democratic values are held, it is difficult to know how this occurs. Courses or curriculums alone do not accomplish it, but teacher competence coupled with other elements of educational quality appears to produce forces in this direction. There is only scant evidence that teachers communicate their own political values in the classroom, and none at all that they do so in an extracurricular environment. Finally, there is some evidence that an indirect process, not involving transmission of political values, does operate in the realm of the same democratic values. Experience with democratic classroom environments appears to produce citizens with democratic orientations toward politics.

With regard to political content input to the schools, it is certain that various agencies try to control schools' political communications. It is further certain that major social forces—beyond the control of any individual or group—operate in such a way as to affect value input. Recruitment patterns affect who teaches and—the evidence is strong—what they teach in the area of regime values, but, once again, it would be premature to assert that this was a pervasive process. Certain kinds of teacher training apparently make teachers willing to express government-level values to their students. This of course does not tell us anything about the expression of particular kinds of government-level values; it indicates only the conditions under which the usual political vacuousness of the schools might be abrogated. Finally, local community features apparently have some bearing on political teaching. Exactly how this comes about is hard to say, though it may involve indirect elite influences.

The over-all impact of this research is at once disappointing and stimulating. On the disappointing side, despite their great socialization potential, schools have not been thoroughly investigated. This is especially true with regard to their role in government-level values and substantive regime considerations. The focus on democratic values seems excessive. Also, the available data have a curiously inconclusive tone; perhaps it would be wise to look elsewhere for important agents of childhood socialization. On the bright side, many of the potential impacts of the school depend on consensual values or widespread social practices. It is very difficult to test for these. But we are in a period of rapid social change. Many aspects of educational systems in the modern world will certainly undergo modification in the near future. If the schools are, in fact, important socializers, their changing nature should be reflected in the political socialization of the young. The future will be revealing.

SOCIALIZATION AT THE COLLEGE LEVEL

Many of the questions and problems surrounding college-level socialization are essentially the same as those dealing with the school. Although colleges are not so likely to be considered civic training institutions, some people may fear that insidious professors or evil books may politically subvert the young. Like the schools, colleges offer a great deal of instruction with specifically political content. It is only natural that we should also wonder what the behavioral consequences of that instruction might be. Scholars of college political socialization, like those of the schools, seem particularly concerned with democratic participatory values; however, there are some important differences in the ways they have approached these problems. Furthermore, some different apparent socialization mechanisms exist, and some obvious political behaviors of college students do not have counterparts at the school level. Therefore a separate look at the college is justified.

Perhaps the most dramatic and visible political phenomenon on today's college campus is the activist student. Campus political activism, long observed in many countries, has appeared with dramatic speed on the American scene in recent years. Immediately, questions of political socialization come to mind. Why should students be so much more involved than their nonacademic contemporaries? What is the source of their generally "anti-establishment" political values? That college-related influences may be at work here is a possibility that cannot escape the notice of any serious observer.[37]

Because colleges in many ways are quite different from schools, we may use a different set of concepts in determining what we wish to know. We could, of course, use the same scheme as we did for schools, but the greater degree of control that individual college professors exercise over their own courses makes some elements of that scheme less useful. Further, college provides a greater diversity of noninstructional experiences than schools typically do; it is altogether possible that these experiences may have some political socialization consequences. Accordingly, it seems best to proceed with a somewhat simpler set of concepts in examining college political socialization.

Modes of College Political Socialization: Two Concepts. There are two basic ways in which college might be considered a socializing agent: as a pervasive environmental context and as an inculcator of specific political values. On the one hand, college is a four-year, many-faceted event. College education is a composite term for many things; information and critical capacities are supposedly acquired; modes of meeting problems are learned; patterns of social interaction likely to last a lifetime are begun. Such a pervasive and dramatic experience is certain to have some lasting impact, and this impact may sometimes have political components.[38] On the other hand, one can think of college as providing specifically politically relevant instruction. There are courses with overt political content in several of the social sciences, and even in the humanities. Moreover, some of that instruction is apparently offered not only in the hope that students' knowledge will be expanded, but also with the desire to manipulate student values.[39] In short, indoctrination may be attempted, whether it is aimed at inducing people to participate in conventional political activity, at stimulating support for partisan alternatives, or at encouraging interest in radical programs and methods.

Obviously, these two ways of acting as a socialization agent are not conceptually distinct. The first merely regards college as an undifferentiated stimulus, while the second looks at an identifiable element of that stimulus. Part of the over-all college experience is instructional, but this is surely not the only part that may have political consequences.

Content of College Socialization: Two Types. There are also two basic kinds of political content that colleges and universities have been expected to transmit. First, as already noted, there is the traditional democratic goal of teaching conventional political participation. Producing "better" citizens and encouraging enlightened, educated persons to become actively involved in influencing governmental policy have long been regarded as important regime-level value tasks of colleges.[40] Colleges join the schools in this concern.

Though the tradition out of which this concern grows has been, and continues to be, important, and though much of the research on college socialization has dealt with it, one must realize that its focus is extremely narrow and is of particular significance only for conditions in which there is great unanimity about the desirability of continuing and operating through an existing democratic order. Clearly, particularly among college youth, there is some serious question about whether this order should be maintained. Other regime-level values—more substantive ones—also deserve attention, for even among youth who do not question regime-level values, an interest in participation hardly seems sufficient. *What* is desired—that is, the substance of one's values—is surely just as important as willingness to take some sort of participatory action. Indeed, participation levels may *depend* in part on the nature of preferred substantive values. Thus, there should be some inquiry into government-level values of college youth. Substantive questions of policy among college youth are fully deserving of attention.[41]

Some Areas for Investigation. By a simple cross-classification of these two-fold distinctions, we can identify four interesting areas of investigation. Placing "mode" of college socialization against "content" generates the table on page 116, the cells of which indicate kinds of socialization problems.

What do we know about each of these four kinds of socialization areas? First, looking at Cell A, numerous studies, usually based on surveys of general populations, indicate that college education is in fact associated with high levels of conventional

| | Mode of Socialization | |
Content of Socialization	General College Experience	Specific Political Instruction
Conventional Democratic Participation	A	B
Substantive Political Values (regime and government levels)	C	D

participation in the democratic political process. Activities like voting and other election-related operations are more likely to be performed by college graduates than by less-educated citizens.[42] Though these associations may in fact be spurious (because more active people seek education), it is often argued that there may be something about the college experience that induces greater activity. What that element might be—greater ability to understand the impact of political events upon one's life, increased exposure to stimuli in the form of interpersonal contact or mass media, or some other factor—is not obvious and usually not directly demonstrated. Certainly, few studies show that graduates report being *taught* to be active while in college classes. Thus, research of Cell A, though perhaps it raises more questions than it answers, in general suggests that college has an influence.

Research in Cell B might be able to shed light on the undifferentiated stimulus of college education and its effects on participation; political instruction per se could act as a powerful stimulus to conventional activity. Many scholars have argued that greater knowledge of the democratic political process might increase feelings of efficacy and thus motivation toward participation. And, as noted above, many instructors believe that their role includes political activation of students. In fact, however, direct investigation of university students reveals that exposure to courses with political content of various types appears to produce no increments in participatory tendencies. Measures made before and after taking political science or social sci courses are not significantly different on variables like attitude toward politicians, newspaper reading, and attitude toward (conventional) participation.[43] Indeed, one study showed *decreased* propensities to participate among students after they had been exposed to formal instruction. Although the instructors involved might be vindicated of charges of counterproductive instruction (the author of that study attributes the eclipse of participation to the ebb of excitement about an election held near the time of the initial measurement),[44] one is strongly tempted to entertain the hypothesis that any effects of college education in increasing conventional participation are not dependent upon formal instruction with political content. Indeed, one might argue the counterproposition, that knowledge of the political process is just as likely to make students more cynical and, although perhaps it increases a tendency toward change-oriented political activism, may even *decrease* motivation toward conventional democratic participation. In any event, there is apparently nothing inherently productive of conventional democratic participation in the receipt of politically oriented college instruction in the United States today.

Turning our attention from participation to substantive values, we find reports of positive connections in Cell C between the undifferentiated university experience and change in certain orientations. Although political socialization studies demonstrate that many basic regime and community values are acquired much earlier than the college years, it can again be demonstrated by survey research on general populations that better-educated citizens hold different political values than their less-educated counterparts.[45] For example, a better-educated person is more civil libertarian, in that he is tolerant of the expression of minority political views; and he is more "positive," in that he is not cynical about governmental processes and is less suspicious of government officials. This finding—which suggests that the impact of college is in the same direction as the schools—is reinforced by direct studies of students.

Researchers exploring the possibility of college-induced changes in other kinds of political attitudes have investigated students at various times during, or beyond, their educations. Although often changes attributable to the college experience are minimal,[46] there are clearly circumstances in which substantial changes along some kind of "liberal-conservative" dimension emerge.[47]

The most famous investigation in this area is probably Newcomb's study of Bennington College in the 1930's. Girls, who as freshmen manifested middle-class values typical of their backgrounds, underwent considerable transformation, gradually coming to favor "New Deal" type policy alternatives by the time they were seniors.[48] These findings are the more striking because the changes in the students have largely persisted for twenty-five years.[49] Apparently, the changes during the college years were so monumental that they affected the way in which these students lived their subsequent lives. Of course, such changes could have resulted from the historical experience of living through those difficult times, but this does not appear to have been the case. The college experience seems to have been critical. An exact interpretation of why this college was able to have such a dramatic influence upon these students is not available. As Newcomb indicates, it is impossible to isolate the "causative factors" in the undifferentiated college experience. However, such changes do appear· explicable in terms of social psychological group theory and subscription to community norms. To be sure, faculty may have been prominently involved in this process, but not necessarily through any instructional effort. Faculty at this college determined community norms because of. their high degree of social interaction with the students. The "liberal" political values professed by the faculty were absorbed by students regardless of academic major, suggesting that the content of what was taught was of little importance.[50] Indeed, it might seem more accurate to attribute this student change to a *peer*-mediated phenomenon, for it may be intimate social relationships that are prominently involved. The social basis for the reported student changes is suggested by other evidence from the Bennington study as well. We shall return to a discussion of peers as socialization agents in chapter 6.

For some strange reason, the possibilities of Cell D—that

specific political instruction may affect students' substantive political values—have been almost entirely neglected by researchers. This is ironic, for both popular fear that professors with "subversive" ideas will contaminate innocent youth and a more measured academic interest in the college as political socializer dictate close attention here. Perhaps the failure of instruction to transmit participatory values, for example, might not be repeated in the area of substantive values. Instructors are likely to present substantive imperatives more forcefully than participatory ones. The latter, after all, are instrumental to the former; unless one has some goals to achieve through participation, one is probably not motivated to become actively involved.[51]

Paralleling some of the concerns we discussed in connection with the schools, one study sought to determine (1) whether government-level issue values specifically advocated in the classroom had any impact on students, and (2) whether similar values that professors themselves held had any impact on students. The study compared attitudes of students in different sections of an American government course who had been exposed to professors with different patterns of advocacy and different personal values. The results showed that students' values were unaffected by the political postures of their professors. Students whose instructors advocated social welfare programs were no more favorable to such programs than students of instructors who did not advocate them. Students of radical professors were no more "liberal" and no less supportive of the Vietnam war than students to whom no radical appeals were made. Further, there was no association between professors' own values and those of their students on these very same policy areas.[52] The same study sought to determine whether different teaching content had some unintended value consequences to students. Levels of several regime- and community-support variables (social obligation, attributions of legitimacy) in general did not depend on how students' instructors presented political materials. Thus, though these findings need to be confirmed by additional research, it appears that Cell D does not describe a very important college socialization pattern. Regardless of whether direct value transfer or more indirect processes are considered, college instruction appears to do no better a job of communicating substantive values than it does in transmitting participatory imperatives.

Although the college experience undoubtedly has some political consequences, as revealed by some positive findings in Cells A and B, formal instruction seems to have little impact. Though the professor does not appear to be an effective political manipulator, something does happen to youngsters during their four years of college education. But the "causative agent" is still largely a mystery. Finding that causative agent is a task of first priority. And we have a clue to what it might be. Newcomb's findings (Cell B) suggested an important political socialization role for peer relationships. If the agent is not instructors, it may be friends. We now turn to a more systematic investigation of peer groups as political socializers.

NOTES

1. Gabriel Almond and Sidney Verba, *The Civic Culture* (Boston: Little-Brown and Co., 1965), chaps. 4–7; Lester W. Milbrath, *Political Participation* (Chicago: Rand McNally & Co., 1965) chaps. 4–5.
2. James W. Prothro and Charles M. Grigg, "Fundamental Principles of Democracy: Bases of Agreement and Disagreement," *Journal of Politics*, 23 (May 1960): 276–84; Herbert McCloskey, "Consensus and Ideology in American Politics," *American Political Science Review*, 58 (June 1964): 367–82.
3. These six processes were first set forth and discussed in Dean Jaros and Bradley C. Canon, "Transmitting Basic Political Values: The Role of the Educational System," *School Review*, 77 (June 1969): 94–107.
4. James P. Shaver, "Reflective Thinking, Values and Social Studies Textbooks," *School Review*, 73 (Autumn 1965): 226–57; Byron G. Massialas, "American Government: We Are the Greatest," in *Social Studies in the United States*, C. Benjamin Cox and Byron G. Massialas, eds. (New York: Harcourt, Brace & World, 1967), pp. 167–95.
5. Richard E. Gross and William E. Badger, "Social Studies," in *Encyclopedia of Educational Research*, Chester W. Harris, ed. (New York: Macmillan Co., 1960), pp. 1296–1313.
6. Edgar Litt, "Civic Education Norms and Political Indoctrination," *American Sociological Review*, 28 (February 1963): 69–75; C. Benjamin Cox and Jack E. Cousins, "Teaching Social Studies in Secondary Schools and Colleges," in *New Challenges in the Social Studies*, Byron Massialas and Frederick R. Smith, eds. (Belmont, Calif.: Wadsworth Publishing Co., 1965), chap. 4.
7. Howard E. Wilson, *Education for Citizenship* (New York: McGraw-Hill Book Co., 1938); Roy A. Price, "Citizenship Studies in Syracuse," *Phi Delta Kappan*, 33 (December 1951): 179–81; Earl E. Edgar, "Kansas Study of Education for Citizenship," *ibid.*: 175–78.
8. Kenneth P. Langton and M. Kent Jennings, "Political Socialization and the High School Civics Curriculum," *American Political Science Review*, 62 (September 1968): 858.

9. Gross and Badger, *op. cit.*; Joseph Katz, "The Political and Economic Beliefs of Student Teachers in the Social Studies," *Social Studies,* 44 (April 1953): 142–45.
10. David G. Ryans, "Research on Teacher Behavior in the Context of the Teacher Characteristic Study," in *Contemporary Research on Teacher Effectiveness,* Bruce J. Biddle and William J. Ellena, eds. (New York: Holt, Rinehart & Winston, 1964), pp. 67–101.
11. D. Dee Castetter et al., *Teacher Effectiveness: An Annotated Bibliography* (Bloomington: Indiana University Institute of Education, 1954).
12. Bruce J. Biddle, "The Integration of Teacher Effectiveness Research," in Biddle and Ellena, *op. cit.,* pp. 1–40; Hazel Davis, "Evolution of Current Practices in Evaluating Teacher Competence," in *ibid.,* pp. 41–66.
13. Richard M. Merelman, *Political Socialization and Educational Climates* (New York: Holt, Rinehart & Winston, 1971).
14. *Ibid.,* p. 108.
15. George D. Spindler, "Education in a Transforming American Culture," *Harvard Education Review,* 25 (Summer 1955): 145–56.
16. Louis E. Raths et al., *Values and Teaching* (Columbus, Ohio: Charles E. Merrill, 1965); Byron G. Massialas and C. Benjamin Cox, *Inquiry into Social Studies* (New York: McGraw-Hill Book Co., 1966), chap. 7.
17. Harmon Zeigler, *The Political Life of American Teachers* (Englewood Cliffs, N.J.: Prentice-Hall, 1967), chap. 4.
18. Mark Chesler, "Values and Controversy in Secondary Social Studies," in Massialas and Cox, *op. cit.,* pp. 270–88; John P. Lunstrum, "The Treatment of Controversial Issues in Social Studies Education," in Massialas and Smith, *op. cit.,* pp. 121–47.
19. Robert D. Hess and Judith V. Torney, *The Development of Political Attitudes in Children* (Chicago: Aldine Publishing Co., 1967).
20. See, e.g., Margaret Willis, *The Guinea Pigs After Twenty Years* (Columbus: Ohio State University Press, 1961), pp. 166, 194–95; William A. Lewis et al., "Interpersonal Relationship and Pupil Progress," *Personnel and Guidance Journal,* 44 (December 1965): 396–401; Robert R. Carkhuff and Charles B. Truax, "Toward Explaining Success and Failure in Interpersonal Learning Experiments," *Personnel and Guidance Journal,* 45 (March 1966): 723–28.
21. Robert W. Frederick, *The Third Curriculum* (New York: Appleton-Century-Crofts, 1959), chaps. 4–5; Morris L. Bigge, "Out of the Classroom Expected Learning Often Comes Through Unexpected Teaching," *Exceptional Children,* 34 (September 1967): 47–50.
22. Albert Bandura, *Principles of Behavior Modification* (New York: Holt, Rinehart & Winston, 1969), pp. 118–204.
23. Hess and Torney, *op. cit.,* pp. 111–15.
24. Massialas and Cox, *op. cit.,* pp. 111–35. This notion has a venerable heritage. See John Dewey, *Democracy and Education* (New York: Macmillan & Co., 1916), pp. 116–67.
25. Almond and Verba, *op. cit.,* chap. 11.
26. Litt, *loc. cit.*
27. Merelman, *op. cit.,* p. 15.
28. Zeigler, *op. cit.,* p. 33.
29. Merelman, *op. cit.,* pp. 205–7.
30. Nolan C. Kearney and Patrick Rocchio, "The Effect of Teacher Education on Teachers' Attitudes," *Journal of Educational Research,* 7 (November 1956): 703; "Teaching Teachers to Provide Liberal Education" (Symposium), *Journal of Teacher Education,* 18 (Summer 1967): 132–33; Massialas and Cox, *op. cit.,* pp. 279–98.

31. M. Kent Jennings and Harmon Zeigler, "Political Expressivism Among High School Teachers: The Intersection of Community and Occupational Values," in *Learning About Politics,* Roberta Sigel, ed. (New York: Random House, 1970), p. 445.
32. Dean Jaros, "Transmitting the Civic Culture: The Teacher and Political Socialization," *Social Science Quarterly,* 49 (September 1968): 292.
33. Merelman, *op. cit.,* p. 164.
34. Jennings and Zeigler, *op. cit.,* pp. 439–43.
35. Zeigler, *op. cit.,* p. 128; Jaros, *op. cit.,* pp. 288, 294.
36. Neal Gross, *Who Runs Our Schools?* (New York: John Wiley & Sons, 1958), p. 20.
37. Seymour Martin Lipset, ed., *Student Politics* (New York: Random House, 1967); Joseph W. Scott and Mohammed El-Assal, "Multiversity, University Size, University Quality and Student Protest: An Empirical Study," *American Sociological Review,* 34 (October 1969): 702–9.
38. Alex S. Edelstein, "Since Bennington: Evidence of Change in Student Political Behavior," *Public Opinion Quarterly,* 26 (Winter 1962): 564–65.
39. Marian Schick and Albert Somit, "The Failure to Teach Political Activity," *The American Behavioral Scientist,* 6 (January 1963): 5–7.
40. Thomas H. Reed and Doris D. Reed, *Evaluation of Citizenship Training and Incentive in American Colleges and Universities* (New York: Citizenship Clearing House, 1950); Earl Latham, Joseph P. Harris, and Austin Ranney, *College Standards for Political Science: A Policy Statement* (New York: Citizenship Clearing House, 1959).
41. Kenneth Prewitt and Joseph Okello-Oculi, "Political Socialization and Political Education in the New Nations," in Sigel, ed., *op. cit.,* pp. 607–21; Kenneth Keniston, *Young Radicals* (New York: Harcourt, Brace & World, 1968); Russell Middleton and Snell Putney, "Student Rebellion Against Parental Political Belief," *Social Forces,* 41 (May 1963): 383–86.
42. There is a vast literature establishing this point. For a resume, see Milbrath, *op. cit.,* pp. 122–24. However, note that this finding may be peculiar to modern, Western cultures. Contrary findings are reported in Appleton, "The Political Socialization of Taiwan's College Students, *Asian Survey,* 10 (October 1970): 910–23, and M. Lal Goel, "The Relevance of Education for Participation in a Developing Society," *Comparative Political Studies,* 3 (October 1970): 333–46. Thus, some feature peculiar to Western education seems to produce the participatory result. This only underscores the importance of research that abstracts the educational experience into constituent parts and seeks the influence of each.
43. Schick and Somit, *op. cit.*; Albert Somit et al., "The Effect of the Introductory Political Science Course on Student Attitudes Toward Personal Political Participation," *American Political Science Review,* 52 (December 1958): 1129–32.
44. Charles Garrison, "Political Involvement and Political Science: A Note on the Basic Course as an Agent of Political Socialization," *Social Science Quarterly,* 49 (September 1968): 305–14.
45. Prothro and Grigg, *op. cit.*; McCloskey, *op. cit.* Bernard Berelson et al., *Voting* (Chicago: University of Chicago Press, 1954), p. 334.
46. Philip E. Jacob, *Changing Values in College* (New York: Harper & Brothers, 1957), p. 50; Walter T. Plant, "Longitudinal Changes in Intolerance and Authoritarianism for Subjects Differing in Amount of College Education over Four Years," *Genetic Psychology Monographs,* 72 (November 1965): 277–82.

47. Nevitt Sanford, ed., *The American College* (New York: John Wiley & Sons, 1962); Reo M. Christenson and Patrick J. Carpetta, "The Impact of College on Political Attitudes: A Research Note," *Social Science Quarterly*, 49 (September 1968): 315–20.
48. Theodore M. Newcomb, "Attitude Development as a Function of Reference Groups: The Bennington Study," in *Readings in Social Psychology*, Eleanor S. Maccoby et al., eds., 3d ed. (New York: Holt, Rinehart & Winston, 1958), pp. 266–67.
49. Theodore M. Newcomb et al., *Persistence and Change: Bennington College and Its Students After Twenty-Five Years* (New York: John Wiley & Sons, 1967), pp. 39–40.
50. *Ibid.*, p.
51. Milbraith, *op. cit.*, p. 53.
52. Dean Jaros and R. Darcy, "The Elusive Impact of Political Science: More Negative Findings," *Experimental Study of Politics*, 2 No. 1, 14–54.

6. *The Socializers: Peer Groups*

The last two chapters, although they say a great deal about the socialization of youth to politics today, have a decidedly inconclusive and qualified character to them. It is evident that the ability of both family and school to implant political values in children is severely limited. Indeed, the accelerated erosion of traditional institutions—including family, school, and church—is a central feature of the modern age. The socialization potential of such groups has been reduced by increasing competition. Thus, it is not surprising that today we should find family and school but limited instruments of political socialization.

The modern-day competitors of the family and schools are easy to discover. The wealth and technology of modernity have had two dramatic effects on virtually everyone in the world. They have greatly increased the quantity and variety of communications received, and they have greatly increased the number and variety of personal contacts experienced. Electronic communications and publications leave virtually no one untouched today, while in a previous era even the basic communication skill of literacy was rare. Years ago, most people were restricted to contacts largely within their families, but today physical mobility imposes no such limitations; modern man ranges far and wide, encountering others and acquiring new peers, i.e., friends and associates who have similar life circumstances. Of course, young people have fewer ties to the traditions and therefore are the most likely to be susceptible to the new forces.

Thus, there are two broad categories of modern influences on the political socialization process: mass-mediated communication and direct personal contacts through peer groups. It is to the possible political influence of peer groups that the remainder of this chapter is devoted. Putting aside a discussion of mass communication should not be interpreted to mean that it is unimportant. Indeed, mass communication and its impact on political behavior must be investigated thoroughly. However, perhaps precisely because of the great breadth of its possible effects, it has not been dealt with in a political socialization context. Accordingly, it is appropriate to leave this field to more explicit treatment by specialists in political communications. Moreover, it should be noted that it seems quite likely that whether a youngster pays any attention to the mass media is in part dependent upon his peer group relationships. Some research suggests that the political content of the mass media really reaches relatively few persons, and that these people, acting as leaders among their peers, relay the content and their interpretation of it to others. This is called the "two-step flow of communication hypothesis." If it operates in this fashion, peer groups are essential links in how the media make their influence felt. A prior interest in peer groups is thus altogether justified.

Once again, we have an agent—the peer group—that is probably heavily involved in the socialization of the young. Once again, we must ask whether there are any political components (as seems likely) to this socialization and, if so, by what processes it proceeds. Here may lie part of the answer to the problems raised by chapter 3; here may be a partial understanding of the limited nature of family and school socialization.

THE PROCESSES OF PEER SOCIALIZATION

The phenomenon of a young person rejecting the values of his parents in favor of those of his friends is common. Although something of this happens in most normal maturational processes without much substantive effect, acute instances of it, particularly among mobile groups, may be extremely significant. Intrafamily conflict over this kind of development is frequent in legend and literature, to say nothing of real-life instances we all know of. Similarly, given the findings in chapter 5, it takes only a little cynicism to think that many schoolchildren are much more moved by their classmates than by teachers or the program of instruction. A dichotomy between a formal and somehow false and inefficacious program of instruction on the one hand and informal but relevant and meaningful learning experiences outside the classroom is one that is frequently posed. Current contrast of regular university curriculums with those of simultaneously present "free universities" is a case in point.

But even if these remarks suggest strong peer influence, we may further ask how it comes about. Four processes can be envisioned. First, and rather ironically, considering what has been said so far, peers need not represent a challenge to family and school. In homogeneous cultures, peers may be the agencies through which the prevailing values are more effectively transmitted and reinforced. Second, peers may act to instill values particular to a given segment of the population. Simply, a group may communicate its majority political position to members who do not originally hold that position. Third (and this is particularly relevant for young people), groups of peers may develop new and distinctive subcultures of their own, with peculiar associated values. New political positions are created as a new group emerges. Fourth, there may be a process involving no direct value transfer, such as those we discussed with respect to parents and schools. That is, nonpolitical features of groups—for example their authority structures—may affect members in ways that have consequences for political behavior.

Peers as Transmitters of Prevailing Culture. The great influence of groups on the political opinions and behavior of their members is well documented in political science research. Because such groups control much that individuals desire—personal interaction, approval, affection, and prestige—their influence is easy to understand. Not only do groups succeed in transmitting idiosyncratic government-level values—party identification is one—but they may also transmit broadly shared consensual political values at the level of the regime or community. There is evidence, for example, that citizens who belong to few groups, who are socially unintegrated, may lose feelings of efficacy in democratic politics, may support political extremism, or may become especially rejective of referendum proposals.[1] Also, political participation clearly drops off among such people.[2] This is frequently interpreted with the help of the concept of *alienation*. This complex notion centers around the idea of isolation and estrangement. Perhaps partly because of lack of group contact, people become estranged along a variety of dimensions; this estrangement leads in turn to the "deviant" political behavior and attitudes just discussed.[3] On the other hand, those who have more extensive contact with peers are more likely to absorb consensual norms and to feel efficacious.

We might expect to find evidence of similiar peer processes among children. We have already seen how more totalitarian regimes establish youth groups, with the express purpose of helping to transmit the prevailing political dogma to the young. Surely one of the most visible—and from all accounts the most successful—recent examples of this was the creation of the Red Guard in China. Apparently, Maoists felt that youth needed to be actively involved in the "Great Cultural Revolution" of the late 1960's. By creating an activist youth movement, Chinese superrevolutionaries could achieve three goals: they could generate great commitment on the part of the young for new and far-reaching changes; they could thus create enthusiastic organization for the implementation of these goals, particularly those involving more violent and destructive actions; and they could symbolize the basic features of the Great Cultural Revolution—the destruction of the old and the establishment of the new—by encouraging a youthful group to attack older persons and institutions.[4]

In a less overt way, organizations like the Boy Scouts or the Order of Demolay might be thought to have somewhat the same function even in more democratic states. But over and above this kind of influence, simple peer association may bring one more in contact with society-wide political values and encourage their adoption.

However, the actual evidence that the latter process operates among children is weak. Specifically addressing the possibility that children who have active peer relationships more readily learn consensual norms, a recent study of U.S. second- through eighth-graders found that such social activity had no effect on basic attachment to the political system, most norms of citizen behavior, or compliance to political authority.[5] On the other hand, peer group memberships did appear to influence the youngsters' regime-level participatory values. Greater political discussion, attention to candidates, and greater feelings of political efficacy characterize those students who have more contacts with their cohorts. To be sure, political participation is a widespread political value in this country (even if honored more in word than in deed), and it is possible that youngsters learn these prevailing norms from peer contacts. However, as we shall see shortly, there is another, more plausible, interpretation of the meaning of this kind of peer group influence. We must conclude that, so far as present evidence allows us to tell, peers are apparently not very good at transmitting consensual political values about compliance or participation.

Peers and Particular Political Values. The great effect of peer groups on the political attitudes of their members has perhaps most frequently been noted with regard to *dissensual* values —typically government-level concerns over matters like party differences and disagreement over specific issues.[6] Political divisions in our society are frequently explained in terms of group memberships. This suggests that, even among adults, peer groups may act as important socializers. Somehow, groups induce their members to adopt group-appropriate political values.

Of course, the family itself is an important group, which can be expected to have dramatic political impact on its members, especially while they are still children. Our interest here, however, is in possible competitors to the family in the form of youngsters' age cohorts. Upon reaching adulthood, many do abandon parentally acquired values in favor of others. But an intriguing question is how this kind of "competition" goes on during childhood and youth itself.

It does not tax our powers of imagination to think that peer relationships become very influential among college youth. However, most evidence suggests that college experiences do not rework youth so that their initial characteristics are totally obliterated; what an individual is when he enters college accounts for most of what he is when he leaves. But some change does occur during these years. Moreover, it appears that peer groups are more important in changing college youth than is formal instruction,[7] a suggestion consistent with the findings of chapter 5. There we saw that girls from conservative, middle-class families were induced in the course of four years at a college with a decided liberal atmosphere to change their political policy preferences along a variety of dimensions. These changes, which were permanent, apparently resulted from resocialization through personal contacts with students (true peers) and faculty who entered into informal, peerlike relationships.[8]

But it is entirely possible that peer relationships can begin to subvert parental-mediated values far earlier than the college years. This less apparent possibility was specifically investigated by Langton. He showed that among his sample of Jamaican high school students, political values were associated with social-class characteristics of the students' families. Resembling their cohorts in the United States, students whose parents have relatively low-prestige occupations and relatively little education were less committed to many regime-level democratic values, less supportive of minority rights, less politically involved, and less interested in voting. The lower-class students were also more supportive of the regime than were their higher-class counterparts.

If lower-class youngsters associate with lower-class peers—and if peers, in fact, have political socialization capabilities—we would expect these characteristic lower-class political values to be reinforced; on the other hand, should lower-class youngsters associate with upper-class peers, their political values should show some modification in the direction of those typical of the upper classes. Langton compared working-class students who claimed to have working-class friends with working-class students who claimed to have higher-class friends. Indeed, the two groups differed in the expected way along a variety of dimensions. Those who associate with upper-class youngsters are more positive toward the act of voting, more supportive of political rights for minorities, and less supportive of the regime. The latter result, it might be noted, occurs in direct opposition to the regime-supported urgings of civics textbooks to which these high school youths are exposed. Peers appear more powerful than curriculum as socializers.[9]

Thus, it appears that groups can and do politically socialize not only adults but also college-age youth and even younger students. This is a finding of some significance for several reasons. First, groups are somewhat subject to deliberate manipulation. If group life of youngsters can be controlled, and we have seen that it has been attempted, the controllers may enjoy great political power. Second, as society changes, different interests arise. Groups who share new concerns develop, while those organized around a dying institution atrophy and disappear. The total configuration of peer groups is constantly changing. If groups can induce conformity among their members, they may exert a considerable political force, as the literature on pressure groups tell us. Thus, knowledge of the nature of group life in a country—coupled with the realization that these groups have considerable socialization capability—would do much to aid in understanding the dynamics of politics.

The Creation of Subcultures. If groups are important for the process of political socialization of children and youth, it becomes important to inquire into the sources of the values that relevant groups hold. As we have just seen, the sources can be quite various. Typical liberal values professed by intellectuals seem to have been involved in the example of the resocialized college girls, and social class seems to have generated the orientations of the Jamaican youth. Youngsters' groups could become associated with almost any set of familiar political values. Of some interest, however, is the possibility that groups of youngsters today may constitute themselves into relatively independent subcultures. Peculiar problems and needs may confront young people *as young people,* not as members of any other group, such as intellectuals or the working class. Being young or, alternately, being a student, may be of singular significance in the contemporary era. Not only is there less strong and certain guidance from traditional adult sources today, but also the mass media encourage youngsters to emphasize their youth and to contrast themselves to their elders. This in turn is largely due to the fact that young people, because of general high degrees of affluence in our society, possess and spend great quantities of money. In an attempt to tap this spending potential, it is inevitable that the media should encourage youth to think of themselves as distinctive.

In addition, one could argue that young people as a group share more objective interests today than ever before. First, in the United States, the military draft has been a heated issue for the duration of the nation's longest and most controversial war, Vietnam. More importantly, many youngsters, far more than ever before, are university and college students. With great numbers of people more or less similarly affected by considerations not only of receiving instruction, but of residency, social interaction, and all that these entail, it is not at all surprising that some sense of pervasive interest should arise.

Thus, it may be that today being young involves a sense of cultural identity that is just as real as that which characterizes a social class or an ethnic population in America. Youth culture, although the term is overused, may deserve equal status with ethnic or class culture.

The notion of youth or student culture is—at least in its non-political aspects—by no means new. Specific interests, needs, and demands have been observed along a variety of dimensions, particularly those having to do with coping with the educational establishment.[10] Given the increasing public policy relevance of some of these characteristic youthful concerns, for example, sources of financial aid and priorities of universities, it is altogether reasonable to expect that the youth culture would develop some characteristic political values as well. Indeed, in the great outpouring of literature on contemporary student political activism, a number of findings attribute heightened radical involvement to something like student culture.[11] The great, nationwide student protest in France during 1968 is an interesting case in point. Although there was student unrest throughout Europe at the time, it was particularly pronounced in France. A convincing interpretation of this emphasizes the relatively large student population in France. Unlike most other European countries, nearly 20 per cent of the relevant age group enters the university. Like most countries, France has undergone great social change in recent decades, but, it is argued, the French university system has not kept pace. As a consequence, a significant proportion of the population—the student body—found that it had interests relating to employment and position in a technologically changing society that their institutions were not serving. The resulting uniquely student demands urged both educational and broader political reform.[12] Though this is by no means the only interpretation of today's campus activism, and though the evidence is suggestive at best, the subcultural interpretation is one that deserves our attention. Particularly if student political demands appear to remain fairly consistent over time and do not vary greatly as new techniques of youthful political expression develop, the notion of subculture may add significantly to our understanding of political socialization.

Peer Group Activity and Political Activity. Given the tremendous interest in democratic political participation, peer groups, like all potential agents of political socialization, must be examined for their possible impact in this area. We have already seen how participation plays a role in some of the direct value transfer processes by which peers may operate. But in addition, as elsewhere, we must ask whether participatory habits learned in peer groups are somehow later transferred to the political context. The question has generally been answered in the affirmative. Adults who claim to have opportunities to participate in job decisions in work groups also display greater feelings of political participatory competence.[13] This may indicate that adults who have some feelings of control over aspects of their day-to-day lives generalize them to include beliefs in their own political ability.

Does this indirect socialization process also operate during youth and childhood? Again, it is almost an article of faith with educators that participation in extracurricular activities teaches children feelings of social efficacy, which are then applicable to politics. Ziblatt investigated high school students in an attempt to determine whether such activities did indeed affect political competence. His findings indicated that this kind of peer participation had only an indirect relationship to political norms.[14] Although there might indeed be an association, it is not by a simple process of generalizing participation in a peer group to participation in politics. On the other hand, as we mentioned earlier a study of second through eighth grade youngsters revealed that those who joined groups participated more in a variety of political activities, like discussion, and had more participatory attitudes.[15] Rather than learning the participatory political norms from their peers, this study suggests, group-joining youngsters may learn group participatory skills, which are applied to politics. The data are consistent with such a transfer hypothesis.

Though these findings must be regarded with caution (e.g., it could be that people learn participatory norms elsewhere and then apply them both to peer groups and to political situations), there is again some evidence that an indirect political socialization takes place. Like other agents, peers may equip youngsters with skills that have great political utility.

THE IMPLICATIONS OF PEER GROUP SOCIALIZATION

It has sometimes been said that the study of political socialization, by concentrating on such institutions as families and schools, emphasizes how the traditions and norms of the past may be implanted in today's generation. If inadequate attention to the political world of today and to political change are the result, the problem could be corrected by looking at peer groups, perhaps the ultimate modern agent of socialization. Groups are known to have powerful influence over political attitudes in most circumstances; indeed, they probably play a role in communicating traditional political orthodoxies. But given the conditions of the modern age, peer groups seem to have most prominence as competitors to traditional socialization agents. It is likely that there will be much less continuity in typical government-level values (e.g., parents probably will not be able to communicate as frequently their party identification or views on issues of the day to their offspring) simply because increased peer contact increases the likelihood of exposure to alternate views.

But probably more significant is the possibility that relatively independent subcultures will form among youth in today's world. Such subcultures may develop and enunciate new political values. Thus, not only may peer groups inject some uncertainty into the intergenerational socialization process, but they may introduce altogether unfamiliar substance. This portends very great change in political values—and adds uncertainty in the realm of the usually more consensual community and regime areas as well as at the government level.

Although, as indicated by the relative length of this chapter, not much research has been done on peer groups as political socializers, the little evidence that exists has a positive ring. Surely, greater attention will be given to peers as transmitters and creators of political norms, for some very important political socialization dynamics may be discovered here, and they may well provide a key to understanding how political change takes place. Our need to understand more of what is happening is as obvious as it is important.

NOTES

1. Gabriel Almond and Sidney Verba, *The Civic Culture* (Boston: Little, Brown & Co., 1965), chaps. 9–10; Joel D. Aberbach, "Alienation and Political Behavior," *American Political Science Review,* 63 (March 1969): 86–91.
2. Lester W. Milbrath, *Political Participation* (Chicago: Rand McNally & Co., 1965), pp. 78–81.
3. Ada W. Finifter, "Dimensions of Political Alienation," *American Political Science Review,* 64 (June 1970): 389–410.
4. See an interesting interpretation of the Red Guard movement in Robert Jay Lifton, *Revolutionary Immortality* (New York: Random House, 1968), pp. 31–41; for a fascinating biography of a youth involved in the Red Guard movement, see Gordon A. Bennett and Ronald N. Montaperto, *Red Guard* (Garden City, N.Y.: Doubleday & Co., 1971).
5. Robert D. Hess and Judith V. Torney, *The Development of Political Attitudes in Children* (Chicago: Aldine Publishing Co., 1969), pp. 120–25.
6. Robert Putnam, "Political Attitudes and the Local Community," *American Political Science Review,* 60 (September 1966): 640–55; Anthony Orum and E. McCranie, "Class, Tradition, and Partisan Alignments in a Southern Urban Electorate," *Journal of Politics,* 32 (February 1970): 156–76.
7. Theodore M. Newcomb and Everett K. Wilson, *College Peer Groups* (Chicago: Aldine Publishing Co., 1966), chap. 1.
8. Theodore M. Newcomb, "Attitude Development as a Function of Reference Groups; The Bennington Study," in *Readings in Social Psychology,* Eleanor E. Maccoby et al., eds., 3d ed. (New York: Holt, Rinehart & Winston, 1958), pp. 266–67; Theodore M. Newcomb et al., *Persistence and Change: Bennington College and Its Students After Twenty Five Years* (New York: John Wiley & Sons, 1967), pp. 39–40.
9. Kenneth P. Langton, *Political Socialization* (New York: Oxford University Press, 1969), chap. 5.
10. Walter L. Wallace, *Student Culture* (Chicago: Aldine Publishing Co., 1966); Ernest A. Smith, *American Youth Culture: Group Life in a Teenage Society* (New York: Free Press, 1962).
11. Seymour Martin Lipset and Philip G. Altbach, "Student Politics and Higher Education in the United States," in *Student Politics,* Seymour

Martin Lipset, ed. (New York: Basic Books, 1968), p. 223; Richard E. Flacks, "The Liberated Generation: An Exploration of the Roots of Student Protest," *Journal of Social Issues,* 23 (July 1967): 70; Charles A. Reich, *The Greening of America* (New York: Bantam Books, 1971), pp. 141–70.

12. Raymond Boudon, "Sources of Student Protest in France," in *The New Pilgrims: Youth Protest in Transition,* Philip G. Altbach and Robert S. Laufer, eds. (New York: David McKay Co., 1972), pp. 297–310.
13. Almond and Verba, *op. cit.,* pp. 294–97.
14. David Ziblatt, "High School Extracurricular Activities and Political Socialization," *The Annals,* 361 (September 1965): 20–31.
15. Hess and Torney, *loc. cit.*

7. Political Socialization Theory

After our survey of the study of political socialization, we need to take stock of the enterprise, to examine where students of political socialization have been and where they are going. The final two chapters of this book are devoted to this purpose.

First, as to where we have been, it is clear that political socialization has been given the highest priority by both political philosophers and statesmen since the dawn of recorded history and undoubtedly before. Nearly all of these commentators seem to have shared two assumptions: that political socialization of the young directly and significantly affects the survival potentials of communities, regimes, or governments; and that the processes of political socialization are so straightforward that virtually any agent can transmit values with relative ease. Indeed, these assumptions are still present in popular observations about the political education (or miseducation) of children and youth. Since political socialization has been so universally respected and so universally attempted, it is only natural that modern, empirical political scientists should also consider it important.

During the last twenty years or so, a considerable amount of careful research has been done on political socialization, generating for the first time appreciable evidence bearing on these two classic assumptions. Perhaps the central over-all finding of this research has been that despite its ancient and universal credentials, the second of the two assumptions is not entirely valid: the processes of political socialization are extremely *complex*. It is not necessarily the case that if a child is simply exposed to some political imperative, he will somehow dutifully absorb it. The assumption that children can be educated to politics in a simple way is likely to waste time; indeed, the futility of today's high school civic education is a perfect example of such an error.

The other assumption—that socialization of citizens affects the features of whole political systems—generally appears to be true on the basis of available evidence. But even this is an unsatisfactory finding; for the most part, it leaves unanswered the highly intriguing questions of how, why, and under what circumstances it is true.

In other words, the accumulated wisdom of political socialization consists of many ancient and largely unverified principles of political thought, many unproven though widely shared assumptions, half-true empirical generalizations, and, derivative from the rest, a long list of socialization processes that *might* be operative but about which there is no evidence. Although our survey of political socialization has revealed much that is important, there is also a sense of tentativeness, an awareness that the knowledge we have is terribly incomplete. As with most young sciences, political science—and in particular the study of political socialization—is more characterized by what is unknown and yet to be discovered than by a reliable body of verified knowledge. In this sense, our study is unlike physics and chemistry, which, based on several centuries of systematic empirical investigation, are much more highly developed sciences.

Clearly, as we have emphasized many times in the course of this book, this weakness of political socialization knowledge can be corrected only by additional research and discovery. But if we are ever to have a sensible, integrated body of knowledge, our research cannot proceed on a haphazard, hit-or-miss basis. It must have direction and purpose. Where can we hope for such guidance? The answer is the same as it has been for all other sciences: empirical theory. Quite likely, sixteenth-century chemistry was in a state of incompleteness and disarray similar to that which now besets political socialization. The development of that science was unquestionably greatly aided by theory. We might well profit by this lesson. And one thing is certain: recent empirical research has cast sufficient doubt on some of the classical wisdom about political socialization to justify increased efforts. to understand this subject through empirical theory.

Unfortunately, the word *theory* has many meanings—especially as it applies to politics. Sometimes theory is used to indicate something that is not known: "It is my theory that the President will ask for a tax increase." A "theory and practice" or "theory and fact" dichotomy is commonly used: "In theory, courts of law do not make public policy; in fact, they do." Theory sometimes refers to how things ought to be, to a series of moral judgments. Communist theory asserts the desirability of working-class revolution.

However, to the scientist, be he chemist, physicist, meteorologist, or political scientist, a theory is a series of statements that suggest how certain aspects of the real, or empirical, world relate to one another. Theories are *conceptual;* that is, they are creatures of the mind. The atomic theory of matter, of great importance to physicists and chemists, suggests that the elements composing the universe have atomic numbers, atomic weights, valence, and so on, and that because of these features the elements behave in particular ways. No one has ever seen an atomic number or a valence; these are entirely the product of human invention and thus are theoretical. But if a chemist allows these notions to guide his thinking, he can make sense out of the welter of statements about chemical substances that are known to be true. No student who has ever attempted chemistry can deny that the basic notions of the atomic theory organize and make sense out of the thousands of possible chemical equations. Remembering each chemical equation as an arbitrary fact is clearly impossible. But by depending on the periodic table to make some order out of them in terms of this theory, we can better understand the physical world.

Equally important, theory helps to direct new research. Chemists are deeply engaged in discovering new information about the world. But where and how are they to look? They look where the theory suggests. If the world is put together the way atomic theory suggests, then given chemicals should behave in certain ways under certain conditions. It remains for the chemist to test by experimentation whether the chemicals *actually do* behave the way the theory suggests. The theory has done the service of suggesting what research could be done so that the resulting knowledge would fit into a sensible, orderly scheme.

In most fields of human behavioral science, unlike the physical sciences just described, theories are often incomplete and poorly developed. Thus, in a given area of knowledge, one may find several competing theories attempting to explain one phenomenon. This is simply because there is so little knowledge that there is no basis for making a definitive choice between rivals. But theoretical guidance is still essential to the study of socialization, even though having to choose among several competing theories—and incomplete ones at that—complicates the task.

There are many useful theories of human behavior. Among them, for example, is a role theory. The basic premise of this approach is that in every society there are *positions*, e.g., father, teacher, citizen, etc., about which there are widely shared expectations. People in general expect those who occupy the position of father or teacher to do certain things. Persons who occupy positions play the appropriate role by conforming to the expectations that are held for that position. What a person does may be explained in terms of the roles he plays, that is, in terms of the expectations that surround his positions.[1] If this is indeed the way the world is, then we can develop some explicit hypotheses or predictions about what people will do in certain circumstances. Research, then, consists in testing the hypotheses to which the theory has directed us.

Let us examine some of the theories that might be useful to a more complete understanding of political socialization. As indicated in chapter 1, there have been two major categories of concern in current political socialization research: systems- or macro-level effects, and individual- or micro-level concerns. This duality reappears in our discussion of major assumptions that have characterized ages of interest in political socialization. Accordingly, two kinds of theoretical questions should concern us. On the one hand, we need macro-level theory whose "objective would be to demonstrate the relevance of socializing phenomena for the operations of political systems," [2] while on the other we need micro-level theory to illuminate the processes by which individuals are politically socialized.

MACRO-LEVEL THEORY

Macro-level concerns hang on the edges of consciousness of every political socialization researcher, for it is its macro- or systems-level relevance that makes political socialization worth studying. But, like macro-level research, macro-level theorizing is in a relatively undeveloped state. In fact, it is unrealistic at this stage to expect macro-level theory to suggest specific, testable hypotheses. At present, macro-theory can provide some general guidelines for investigation, can suggest where and for what we should look to do profitable research on political socialization.

Easton and Dennis suggest a macro-level approach called "systems persistence theory." [3] According to this theory, a political system is a collection of institutions and processes through which binding decisions are made for a society. National communities are political systems as are states, cities, and so on. Obviously, it is possible to live simultaneously within more than one system. Easton and Dennis suggest that the key question providing guidance for political socialization research should be, What are the conditions under which systems persist, that is, continue to exist over a long period of time? Political systems are always subject to *stress,* according to this scheme, and their ability to persist depends on their skill in responding to the various manifestations of stress. The demands of a sizable but very angry minority might generate a good deal of stress. Of course, handling stress need not involve retrenchment and suppression of the stress-inducing agent (though it might). It could involve a complete change in regime or a revolution to accommodate the producers of stress. The system could avoid complete collapse only by radical change. Stress that threatens the ability of systems to endure can come in many forms, as we shall see. Socialization may affect the system's susceptibility to particular kinds of threat and may also affect a system's ability to deal with stress.

The authors identify several kinds of stress and show how socialization may be relevant to each. Output stress, for example, has to do with lack of obedience, or noncompliance, to the decisions (laws, edicts, other imperatives) that the system puts out. Throughout this book, we have seen many micro-level investigations of compliance. But Easton and Dennis suggest several other interesting questions at the macro-level. How widespread must a disposition to comply be in order for a system to avoid manifestations of stress? To what extent is coercion or force an effective substitute for socialization in the securing of compliance? Stress may also result from lack of support. Support simply means feelings of trust, affection, or confidence toward aspects of the political system. Diffuse or general support is undoubtedly important in system persistence. Socialization of citizens to such supportive beliefs probably enables regimes to weather many bad periods when they cannot produce satisfying policies. But what is the relationship among tangible benefits received, socialization to support, and stress? To what extent does failure to socialize support require a system to maintain an undiminished flow of satisfying policies?

There are other kinds of stress that can be imagined. (For example, the level of demand for public services may exceed the regime's capability to provide them.) Other kinds of socialization-relevant questions arise in connection with such problems. The point, of course, is that thinking of the political world as made up of systems, each governed by a series of stresses that affect their potential for persistence, is productive of new ideas, as well as new questions whose answers may help us toward a better understanding of the relationship between the practices of political socialization and the great society-wide phenomena of politics. In other words, this theory has done its job. It has suggested new questions to investigate and has provided an orderly framework in which to locate the findings. Though very limited, it is a step in the direction of greater macro-level understanding.

MICRO-LEVEL THEORY

Though there is now a considerable body of micro-level political socialization research, much of the early work—and indeed even a considerable portion of the present efforts—is of a highly atheoretical nature. Where the chief goal is to describe rather than explain children's political orientations, the need for theory is not so apparent. Furthermore, since description is an appropriate task in new areas of study, it is not at all surprising that many scholars of political socialization should have paid relatively little attention to theory. Thus, at the micro-level, too, we are confronted with a low level of theoretical development.

However, several promising strands of behavioral science theory have been used to inform research into the political orientations of children. Perhaps the most prominent of these is the psychoanalytic theory, first developed by Sigmund Freud. Indeed, one could argue that the whole idea of searching for the roots of adult political behavior in childhood is psychoanalytic in origin, for it is a prominent principle of this theory that adult behavior is traceable to specific infantile trauma produced by childrearing practices. In broad outline, psychoanalytic theory suggests that every child is born with instinctual drives whose satisfaction is channeled or thwarted according to his parents' demands. This conflict between unconscious needs and restrictions imposed by the "outside" world is an inevitable part of becoming civilized. Severe unresolved conflict (neurosis) may be disabling, but even the behavior of people who apparently function successfully is affected by remnants of this basic conflict.[4] As students of political socialization, we may ask whether empirical evidence justifies attributing political behavior, including "normal" political behavior, to childhood-induced, unconscious inner conflicts.

We sometimes hear that people support "father figures" in politics, that is, that they project favorable feelings (or unfavorable feelings) toward their parents onto political personalities who possess some similar attributes.[5] The same form of inner conflict that supposedly caused a particular orientation to the father recurs when political authority becomes salient. In chapter 4 we discussed the "anxiety hypothesis," an explanation of the generally positive feelings children manifest toward political figures. This hypothesis is explicitly derived from psychoanalytic theory; it argues that high positive affect toward both parent and political leader is a method of dealing with the great tension (anxiety) of contemplating superpowerful beings.[6] Similarly, the "rebellion hypothesis" discussed in chapter 3 has psychoanalytic roots. Conflicts between needs to establish independence or masculinity in adolescence and dependency upon or identification with parents may produce a reaction that is manifested as political rebellion.[7] The conflict between the need to establish autonomy and the early influence of the father seems to loom large in psychoanalytic thinking, and a variety of political attitudinal solutions to it have been suggested.[8] Finally, there has been some work that actually inquires as to whether neuroses (in the psychoanalytic sense) can lead to specific regime-level substantive values. Almond found that rejection of Western regimes in Italy, France, England, and the United States in favor of Communist Party membership was indeed associated with childhood-induced neurotic passivity, dependence, and unconscious self-rejection.[9]

Thus, psychoanalytic theory can be stimulating and useful to the student of political socialization; indeed, it has been. Considering the evidence that the family is involved in a number of indirect processes of political socialization, it is probably wise to consider a theory which has something to say about the nature and impact of parental relations. Starting from psychoanalytically suggested conflicts and anxieties in young people, by deduction we may be able to develop a new set of hypotheses about familial socialization and eventually increase our understanding of it.

Another approach, which even at first glance seems to be intimately involved in processes of political socialization, is learning theory. It is almost a truism that political orientations must somehow be learned by children. Learning, after all, *means* the acquisition of characteristic response to given stimuli.[10] Examining theories of the psychology of learning would appear to be fruitful strategy for advancing our knowledge of political socialization. Indeed, some scholars have explicitly called for such a theoretical effort.[11]

Classical learning theory holds that people learn according to a schedule of rewards or punishments (reinforcement), which they receive following given responses. If an individual's response is rewarded, he tends to repeat the response (learning it), while punishment inhibits future repetitions of the response. If a symbol (unconditioned stimulus) is continuously associated with the receipt of the reward, presently the appearance of this symbol alone is sufficient to elicit the learned behavior.

Pavlov, the famous psychologist, found that dogs could learn to push levers or switches (a response) if this behavior was reinforced with the reward of food. However, if a bell was rung each time the dogs were rewarded, they soon came to associate the sound (conditioned stimulus) with the receipt of food. Soon, the dogs became *conditioned,* that is, whenever they heard the bell, they would push the levers and switches regardless of whether or not these actions were rewarded with food. It is especially interesting that a learner will continue to respond to the conditioned stimulus *in the absence of reward.* Only intermittent payoff is necessary to retain the association between the conditioned stimulus and the performance of the learned behavior. Because the conditioned stimulus is so closely associated with original reinforcement, it may itself take on the character of a reward. That is, the appearance of the symbol (the bell in Pavlov's experiments) may come to be gratifying in itself. It is a secondary reinforcement, in the absence of the primary one. Accordingly, *new* responses may be learned, responses that lead to the receipt of reward in the form of the appearance of the original conditioned stimulus.[12] Pavlov's dogs learned new behavior if they were rewarded with the sound of a ringing bell.

Does this scheme have any utility for the student of political socialization? Can considering the socialization process to be an example of this model lead to any insightful hypotheses? Merelman argues that citizens come to believe that political regimes are legitimate through "a gigantic process of communication and learning."[13] In his scheme, regimes secure compliance on the part of citizens by offering substantively beneficial policies (primary reinforcement). But they associate symbols and institutions of regime (conditioned stimulus) with the policies. Eventually, the appearance of the conditioned stimulus (e.g., flags, anthems, references to "our form of government," the fatherland) is sufficient to evoke compliance with only intermittent policy (primary) reward. Finally, the symbols become gratifying in their own right (secondary reinforcement). The regime can then demand compliance to its directives without supplying any primary reinforcement; it can merely continue to produce the symbols for the citizens.

We must admit that there is much in the childhood socialization literature that is consistent with these schemes. Children do come to value symbols in their own right and do develop attachments without any reference to policy payoffs. It is further apparent that many agencies of socialization do appeal to such symbols as goals in themselves. The utility of such a theory in generating new hypotheses also seems to be very great. Stimuli that we regard as having particular roles as defined by this scheme should affect the degree of legitimacy accorded a regime. Persons who have learned to associate symbols of the regime with whatever good life they enjoy should be more compliant than others, who may have received more tangible policy payoffs from the regime but who have not made the association and thus derive no secondary reinforcement.

An important variant of learning theory stresses the role of imitation. It can be argued that much learning does not proceed according to the paradigm suggested above. In many cases, reinforcement may not be directly experienced. Instead, learners observe others (models) performing successful behavior and simply imitate their example. Any reinforcement involved is vicarious, that is, rewards are observed to come to the model and it is because of these rewards that the learner may imitate his behavior.[14] One study of socialization of college youth hypothesized that in a classroom situation substantive values toward regime and government policy were more likely to be transmitted than participatory values, because substantive values were more susceptible to imitation in that context.[15] Hirsch specifically posited that the impact of various agents of socialization was dependent upon variables that theoretically affect their availability for modeling: e.g., the agents' orientation to political stimuli or their contiguity. At least moderate support for these imitative learning theory hypotheses was found.[16]

Of course, any of a number of theories in addition to these two might provide much needed guidance in political socialization. Cognitive development theory, for example, is frequently mentioned. This notion emphasizes that what a child acquires is heavily dependent upon the cognitive intellectual equipment available to him at various "stages" in the process of development. These stages, which supposedly follow one another in orderly sequence, describe particular levels of ability of readiness,[17] and it is suggested that particular kinds of political learning may occur at each of these stages.[18] Such a scheme is convenient as a device for describing characteristic political orientations of various age cohorts.

Though micro-level theoretical work is not extensive, obviously some opportunities exist. Theories are available for doing what needs to be done—organizing our knowledge and suggesting where new investigation should be undertaken.

POLITICAL SOCIALIZATION THEORY

The theories suggested here are by no means the only ones available, although they do seem to be among the most promising. However, there is no guarantee that future versions of one of them will come to have the universal acceptability that the atomic theory of matter now enjoys. Indeed, we cannot be sure that any theory in the behavioral sciences will achieve that stature. What is important, however, is that *some* useful theoretical approach be employed to guide and direct research. Subsequent theorizing can build upon, modify, and benefit from this foundation.

Much work in political socialization has not been theoretically informed, which is evident from the disorganized state of the literature we have examined in this book. To reverse this disorganization as more information is acquired, some theoretical constraint is necessary. Rather than argue for the superiority or validity of a given theory, we would urge scholars of political socialization simply to add some theoretical component to their thinking.

NOTES

1. Neal Gross, Ward S. Mason, and Alexander W. McEachern, *Explorations in Role Analysis* (New York: John Wiley & Sons, 1965), chaps. 1–2.
2. David Easton and Jack Dennis, *Children in the Political System* (New York: McGraw-Hill Book Co., 1969), p. 18.
3. *Ibid.*, chaps. 1–3.
4. Robert Waelder, *Basic Theory of Psychoanalysis* (New York: International Universities Press, 1960), pp. 35–41.
5. Richard E. Renneker, "Some Psychodynamic Aspects of Voting Behavior," in *American Voting Behavior,* Eugene Burdick and Arthur J. Brodbeck, eds. (Glencoe, Ill.: Free Press, 1959), pp. 403–4.
6. See chapter 4, p. 91.
7. Talcott Parsons, "Psychoanalysis and the Social Structure," in *Essays*

in Sociological Theory, rev. ed. (Glencoe, Ill.: Free Press, 1954), pp. 336–47.

 8. Robert E. Lane, "Political Education in the Midst of Life's Struggle," *Harvard Educational Review,* 38 (Summer 1968): 468–94.

 9. Gabriel A. Almond, "Types of Neurotic Susceptibility," in *Psychology and Politics,* Leroy N. Rieselbach and George I. Balch, eds. (New York: Holt, Rinehart & Winston, 1969), pp. 211–36.

10. Paul H. Mussen et al., *Child Development and Personality,* 2d ed. (New York: Harper & Row, 1963).

11. Roberta S. Sigel, ed. *Learning About Politics* (New York: Random House, 1970), pp. 1–13; Herbert Hyman, *Political Socialization* (New York: Free Press, 1959), pp. 9–10.

12. O. H. Mowrer, *Learning Theory and the Symbolic Process* (New York: John Wiley & Sons, 1960).

13. Richard M. Merelman, "Learning and Legitimacy," *American Political Science Review,* 60 (September 1966): 549.

14. Albert Bandura, *Principles of Behavior Modification* (New York: Holt Rinehart & Winston, 1969), pp. 118–204.

15. Dean Jaros and R. Darcy, "The Elusive Impact of Political Science: More Negative Findings," *Experimental Study of Politics,* 2 No. 1, 14–54.

16. Herbert Hirsch, *Poverty and Politicization: Political Socialization in an American Sub-culture* (New York: Free Press, 1971).

17. Jean Piaget, *The Moral Judgment of the Child* (New York: Free Press, 1955); Lawrence Kohlberg, "Stage and Sequence: The Cognitive Developmental Approach to the Study of Socialization," in *Handbook of Socialization Theory and Research,* David A. Goslin, ed. (Chicago: Rand McNally & Co., 1969), pp. 347–481.

18. Joseph Adelson and Robert P. O'Neill, "The Growth of Political Ideas in Adolescence: The Sense of Community," *Journal of Personality and Social Psychology,* 4 (July 1966): 295–306; Gustav Jahoda, "Children's Concepts of Nationality: A Critical Study of Piaget's Stages," *Child Development,* 35 (November 1964): 1081–92.

8. The Prospects for Progress: A Hopeful but Cautious Conclusion

The general tenor of the field of political socialization is one of excitement, vigor, and growth. There is no question that the concerns of political socialization are of the greatest significance. They relate to the most basic problems of government; both the contemplations of ancient philosophers and the events of contemporary social protest can be discussed in terms of political socialization. Further, scholars have responded to these questions not only with insightful thinking but with a considerable volume of empirical research, so that we are moderately well informed about political socialization. Moreover, even the areas of ignorance offer encouragement. The problems and questions raised by this research are challenging and fairly beg to be answered. Similarly, the considerable confusion and disorganization that characterizes the accumulated wisdom of political socialization does not appear to be an insurmountable liability. All young sciences experience growing pains, but all can develop with maturity and theoretical and conceptual guidance.

However, we would be remiss if we did not point out that—and this is true of all science—there are also severe problems in acquiring knowledge about socialization. We have already touched on some of them, particularly the great labor of performing adequate macro-level research. This and many other problems can ultimately be solved by expending more time and thoughtful effort on the essentially quantitative problems at hand. But in addition, there exists a series of difficulties inherent in political socialization research, difficulties that have plagued all past and present efforts and will probably continue to do so in the foreseeable future. Some of these dilemmas can be overcome only by the most elaborate and generously financed research; all the difficulties must be recognized, and attempts must be made to minimize their effects. These are essentially problems of research method.

There is an important relationship between *what* we know and *how* we found it out. It is clear that not everything we read is the gospel; history is full of incidents—some of them tragic in their ramifications—in which men acted on the basis of information that was carelessly gathered, imperfectly transmitted, or casually interpreted. Less dramatic, but perhaps closer to each of us, is the phenomenon of the rumor, the half-truth in which the untrue "half" increases with successive retellings.

Contemporary political scientists have increasingly recognized that the *methods* with which we approach our study of any subject are crucial to the accuracy of the knowledge we accumulate. Carelessly gathered information is of little use. Thus, our discussion of political socialization would be truly incomplete if we did not pause to consider some of the important problems of *method* involved in research. Methodology is important not merely for the professional researcher; it is also important for anyone who wants to come to an accurate understanding of the world in which he lives.

SIX METHODOLOGICAL PROBLEMS

All research can be methodologically weak if caution is not exercised, but socialization research seems to have more than its share of obstacles in this regard. First, much political socialization research involves youngsters whose intellectual capacities are immature. As we have seen, children as early as second grade are often the subject of today's studies. Can we communicate with, and elicit meaningful responses from, young minds so unfamiliar with the thinking and language of the social scientist? Any researcher must beware of unwittingly creating a communications gap between himself and subjects, particularly unsophisticated ones. The problem is especially acute with children who are not fully familiar with adult modes of reasoning. We must beware of interpreting their responses in terms of concepts that only the sophisticated adult mind can grasp. Socialization research involves more than simple questioning of children. It entails a careful and sensitive solicitation of information in the subjects' terms rather than those of the researcher.

There is also the question of whether youngsters, even if they understand the inquiries put to them, can respond in a reliable manner. That is, are children's political orientations of so little moment to their holders that they are transient and fleeting? We like to think that the responses we receive in research represent relatively permanent states, not essentially random variation. If this is not the case, if a child will indicate positive feelings toward political authority figures on one day, and resentment and hostility the next, there is some serious question about what we are measuring and about the utility of the whole area of investigation. Not only must the student of political socialization determine whether the very young have political sentiments, he must determine how reliably, how consistently over time, they express them. The extent to which this cannot be done is the extent to which we must hold reservations about socialization research.

Closely associated with this is the problem of instrumentation. What kind of questionnaire, interview schedule, or other device should one use to elicit information from children? If children are asked to write responses, care must be taken not to overtax their abilities to express themselves in this way. Composing, and even the physical act of writing, is difficult for many youngsters. Interviewing children to elicit oral responses requires a sensitivity and understanding greater than that necessary for work with adults. Other methods, such as projective techniques, obviously require special interpretive skills.

A second instrumentation problem is that of operationalizing concepts. Suppose we wish to know whether a child is developing a sense of efficacy in politics, a norm that may have great implication for levels of citizen participation. Should we inquire whether the child himself feels efficacious in politics? Probably not, for children are not direct participants in most political processes. We might then inquire about his perceptions of the impact of adult activity, or about anticipations that he may have about his future behavior. It is obvious, however, that evaluations of adults and self-anticipations are different things. How do we wish to treat this concept, and how shall we measure it?

A severe difficulty, and one that runs through much of the existing research, is that of sampling. Clearly, if grossly atypical or peculiar subjects are investigated in any study, the results may be misleading. What we take to be true of people in general may turn out to characterize only a particular category or group. The solution to this difficulty lies in acquiring representative samples. We are all aware of the care taken to get "random" samples in survey research on adults. Unfortunately, comparable samples of children and youth generally have not been available, and criticism of the restricted applicability of political socialization research has resulted.

It is easy to imagine the difficulty of adequate sampling of children. First, children are more sheltered than adults. Parents typically protect them from the outside world, and this includes preventing access of inquisitive researchers. Often the motives of persons seeking to do research on adults are suspect; the problem is compounded when the subjects are children—especially as few nonspecialists would regard political research on youngsters as a particularly important enterprise. A childhood socialization study based on, say, a random national sample of dwelling units would be very difficult to carry out.

The difficulty of securing subjects for political socialization research has led almost all scholars to depend on schools, thus overcoming many of the physical problems of securing access. Moreover, schools have a considerable degree of control over their charges and can insure the cooperation of most children with the research enterprise. Thus, if the blessing of school administrators can be secured, subjects are readily available. But representative samples are not likely to be obtained in this way. First, any given school is not likely to contain children representative of an entire community. Consideration of neighborhood location and districting insure some diversity among schools. Sampling in several schools may solve this problem, but it is expensive and not always possible. School administrators may deny access to some kinds of schools for reasons of convenience, ongoing instructional programs, or fear of repercussions of the research. Within a given school, access to children is likely to proceed on the basis of classes rather than individuals. Again, certain classes are unlikely to be representative of the entire school. Considerations of convenience, program, desire to exhibit the best classes in the school, or manifold other legitimate and illegitimate reasons may govern those classes to which the researcher is given access. The result is, once more, a very atypical group of subjects.

Not only are schools problematical from the standpoint of sampling, but they also provide restrictive theaters for research along other dimensions. Perhaps the most serious of these is that school administrators may insist on reviewing the content of the research. The desire to censor is, in one sense, understandable. Administrators are sensitive to community pressures of many kinds; should a community group take exception to schoolchildren being asked "controversial" questions, considerable difficulty might be generated. Further, administrators and teachers may fear that inquiry of students would reveal weaknesses or failures in the educational process. They may want assurances that the research cannot be used to generate criticism of themselves. Finally, there may be a desire to prevent the students from being exposed to experiences considered undesirable. It might be thought inappropriate to ask children to contemplate the wisdom or competence of local public officials, for example.

Often, research conducted in the schools must be carried out in the presence of teachers. This is unfortunate, for the presence of a teacher can be intimidating and greatly affect subjects' responses. It can create the impression that the teacher is somehow associated with the research and will have access to the responses that each child gives. That children will adjust responses in this context is not hard to imagine. Even if teachers are not present during the actual administration of the research instrument, children may respond to it as if it were a test. They are accustomed to providing "right" answers when questioned and may seek to provide the response they think is expected, not the one that reflects their actual orientations to politics. Convincing children who are lined up in rows of school desks that a research questionnaire is not just another examination is no easy task.

The Prospects for Progress

A fifth problem is one of longitudinality, or individual
development over time. As we have indicated on several
the link between childhood orientation or experience and adu..
political behavior is only tenuously established in the literature;
few have studied the same subjects continuously over time. Typically, we measure subjects at one point in time and make in-
ferences about past experiences or future behavior. But the problem of longitudinality is not restricted to this basic question. Many
of the studies we have examined compare children of different
ages. Any differences are assumed to be due to development that
takes place as one grows older. Strictly speaking, this is an un-
justified inference. If we discover in 1972 that ten-year-olds are
less politically cynical than fifteen-year-olds, can we argue that
cynicism increases with age? No, for it may be that in 1967,
when the fifteen-year-olds were ten, they were exactly as cynical
as they are now. Political conditions in 1967 may have been such
that young children were made cynical and remained so. Their
younger counterparts may have been spared these cynicizing influences and emerged quite different kinds of individuals. Development with age may not have been involved at all.

Of course, this is similar to the question of maturational and
generational effects, which we discussed in chapter 3. But it
remains a considerable problem in socialization research. Longitudinal studies are difficult to conduct: they are more costly, the
length of time required to complete investigations is far longer,
and it may be impossible to locate the same subjects years later.
It may be unrealistic to expect extensive longitudinal research,
and, as long as it is, we must recognize that prevailing methods,
involving only a single point in time, are subject to some severe
qualifications.

Finally, if we are to have truly adequate *knowledge*—particularly as it relates to macro-level questions—it is necessary that we
have research on political socialization taking place in a variety
of political and cultural settings. At best, cross-national comparative research is difficult, but the most intriguing kinds of questions for the student of political socialization involve particularly
knotty problems. A comparison of the processes and effects of
socialization in a democratic country with those of a more
authoritarian nation would be most revealing. It is, of course, in

the latter that political authorities most vigorously pursue the goal of controlling the political socialization of the young. How fascinating it would be to examine the effects of such efforts.

Unfortunately, research access to such political systems is likely to be very limited. Researchers may simply be prohibited from doing any work. Since political socialization (supposedly) is related to political control, and since few people are anxious for the workings of their control to be known, officials in authoritarian countries are not likely to look with favor on studies of this kind. Of course, this kind of restriction can turn up in any political system. After all, it is similar to the impediments that one often finds in doing research in the public schools. Though problems of access are troublesome to all socialization researchers, their greatest effect is undoubtedly in preventing a look at one of the most interesting socialization processes of all—that which takes place in relatively non-democratic nations.

Thus, many of the methods and techniques used in political socialization research pose real obstacles to knowledge. In a sense, these methods make a prisoner of the scholar. Although progress in methodology will eventually lead us out of this prison, it seems that the magnitude of the problems precludes a sudden, massive jailbreak. The best attitude that we can assume at the moment is one of caution and modesty, leading to a realistic appraisal of what can be accomplished within our limited confines.

THE STUDY OF POLITICAL SOCIALIZATION AND THE FUTURE

The methodological considerations we have just discussed can be dealt with. They may impede and limit, but they do not prevent the study of political socialization. They do, however, underscore the point made many times in this book: it is not easy to know about political socialization. It is by now abundantly clear that perseverance, patience, willingness to proceed by small steps and to recognize limitations, and, above all, ingenuity in theory and method are necessary. The reward for such pains is clearly greater understanding of the process that has been our concern throughout this volume.

But we cannot leave this discussion without pushing our inquiry back one more level. If the hard work of acquiring knowledge leads to increased understanding, to what does the increased understanding lead? Why should we put up with all these impediments? Why should we want to undertake the arduous work of researching political socialization?

One could take a cynical view that increased knowledge of socialization processes will make manipulation of the young easier. Established regimes, if they know how socialization works, can operate their indoctrination programs more efficiently. Thus, it could be argued, socialization knowledge helps to perpetuate political orthodoxy and retard social change. This sounds dark and foreboding.

In one sense, it is a legitimate argument. But two caveats might be entered. First, any and all knowledge can be used for destructive purposes and to achieve ends of which one may not approve. But it is doubtful that increases in knowledge have historically been accompanied by decreases in freedom and declines in the human condition. The greatest exploitations of man by man appear to occur in conditions of *ignorance*. The ignorant man or the ignorant society is helpless before the willful few. It does not take much knowledge to engage in exploitation, only the will to dominate others. Indeed, it may be the case that knowledge allows men to escape this condition.

At the present time, there is no question that children are being politically socialized by many different sources; they *are* being manipulated. But we have only a partial view of the process. Perhaps it is a random operation rather than a conscious and comprehensive program of indoctrination, but it is manipulation nonetheless. Increased knowledge of socialization means increased understanding of this process. Increased understanding clearly implies greater freedom from subjection to largely unknown and therefore uncontrollable and irresponsible forces.

Looking at the same dilemma from another standpoint, we can easily see that while increased knowledge may be used for exploitive purposes, improvements in the human condition can be brought about only through the application of knowledge. If a person wishes to reform society, he must convince people of the superiority of his ideals. What better way to accomplish this end than through childhood political socialization. Or, as one observer put it, "the wise citizen and responsible public servant can enjoy unprecedented prerogatives for useful and humane intervention in the evolution of political systems," [1] as a consequence of greater political socialization knowledge. Manipulation, because of its dangers and its benefits, is a sword that cuts two ways.

Of course, these comments inevitably lead to the argument that knowledge is a good thing in itself. If one accepts this proposition, if knowing and understanding human affairs are regarded as ends in their own right, then perseverance in the study of political socialization is especially justified. Despite the difficulties of knowing about socialization, its investigation provides great insights to the politics of all times.

Thus, there is ground for considerable optimism. Regardless of one's interests, one can anticipate particularly interesting and fruitful results to emerge from the study of political socialization.

NOTE

1. Kenneth P. Langton, *Political Socialization* (New York: Oxford University Press, 1969), p. 179.

Index

157